THE SUPERINTENDENT SEARCH PROCESS:

A Guide to Getting the Job and Getting Off to a Great Start

Tim Quinn, Ph.D.

with
Michelle E. Keith

© Quinn and Associates, Ltd.
Old Mission, Michigan

Published by Quinn and Associates, Ltd., PO Box 157, Old Mission, MI 49673
timquinn@omleader.com

Other titles from this author include:

In the Arena: Building the Skills for Peak Performance in Leading Schools and Systems
Peak Performing Governance Teams: Creating an Effective Board/Superintendent Partnership
Within Reach: Leadership Lessons in School Reform from Charlotte-Mecklenburg Schools

These titles, and additional copies of this monograph, are available through major online bookstores.

All profits from the sale of this monograph are dedicated to scholarship programs for high needs youth.

ISBN: 1453886397
EAN-13: 9781453886397

THE
SUPERINTENDENT SEARCH PROCESS:
A Guide to Getting the Job and
Getting Off to a Great Start

<u>**Contents**</u>   <u>**Page**</u>

FOREWORD

This monograph is written for anyone who aspires to the superintendency, as well as anyone already in the superintendency who may decide at some point to pursue another. Sections of the book may also be of particular help to school boards seeking to hire a superintendent, including Overview of the Search Process, Working with the Search Firm, The Superintendent Interview Process, and Superintendent Contract Negotiation. In addition, the chapters on Letters of Application and Resumes, Transition Planning, and Plan of Entry will be useful to leaders entering cabinet level positions in school districts.

The information provided applies to superintendent searches in all types of districts—from rural to urban, small to large, East Coast to West Coast, and North to South. Where differences in the processes, laws or practices exist, I've tried to point them out. But the processes everywhere are typically very similar—it is the pertinent state laws and the politics in each community that may prompt differences in process.

This monograph is written from the perspective of someone who has not only been a school superintendent, but who has worked with school boards to conduct over 150 superintendent searches and coached scores of successful superintendents through the search process, negotiation of their contract, and then through their first year on the job. The guidance provided in this monograph also incorporates the best perspectives of others who have done similar work throughout America.

My purpose is to help candidates understand the entire search process in detail:
- Deciding to pursue the superintendency
- Applying for a specific superintendency
- Crafting the best resume and application materials
- Mastering the interview process from beginning to end
- Negotiating (and the fine points of accepting or rejecting) a superintendent contract offer

Finally, this monograph will help the new superintendent master the critical milestones of Year One on the job—getting it right, from the start.

Tim Quinn

ACKNOWLEDGEMENTS

Any knowledge or wisdom presented in this monograph is a direct result of the experiences I've had in working with aspiring superintendents, great educational leaders, coaches, mentors, and superintendent search consultants. (There are too many to list by name, but you all know who you are.)

The opportunity to work with these leaders, learn from their experiences, and observe them on the job both up close and from afar (at their very best, and sometimes when they've been something less than they aspired to be) has provided the richest learning of my career.

The credit does truly go to those "in the arena." We hope that the information provided herein, based upon their experiences, makes the arena a little less "dusty, sweaty, and bloody" for those who will follow.

I'd like to thank several "critical friends" who reviewed early stages of this monograph and provided feedback and suggestions: Bill Attea, John Dilworth, Pete Gorman, Jim Huge, Nancy McGinley, Bill Newman, Gary Ray, Abelardo Saavedra, Steve Triplett, and Mike Wilmot. Their input made this a much better product.

Thanks, also, goes to our editor John Bebow, for his great work in helping with this writing.

And thanks to my co-author and co-conspirator on this project, Shelley Keith, for putting all this information together in such an organized and accessible piece of work.

In the Arena

It is not the critic who counts, not the man who points how the strong man stumbled or where the doer of deeds could have done them better.

The credit belongs to the man who is actually in the arena; whose face is marred by dust and sweat and blood;

who strives valiantly; who errs and comes short again and again;

who knows the great enthusiasms, the great devotions, and spends himself in a worthy cause;

who, at the best, knows the triumph of high achievement;

*and who, at the worst, if he fails, at least fails while daring greatly,
 so that his place shall never be with those cold and timid souls
who know neither victory nor defeat.*

   -    *Theodore Roosevelt, 1910*

Message
From a Child in a Failing School
To Future School Leaders

Whisper in My Heart

So it tells me that you're coming,
This whisper in my heart.
It tells me that you're coming
To take this place apart.

So it tells me that you're brave,
It tells me that you're smart.
It tells me you'll be strong,
This whisper in my heart.

So it tells me I deserve you
That I, too, am smart and strong.
It tells me that you'll save me
As these whispers rise to song.

So it tells me that you're coming
To save me from this fate.
I hope that you will hurry—
I pray you're not too late!

INTRODUCTION

Intentional and successful navigation of the search process lays the ground work for a superintendent's ultimate success on the job. Careful management of each step in the process will impact your work in the following ways:

- Thorough preparation will prevent you from being thrust into a role you aren't ready for—or one for which you may be overqualified.
- Thoughtful consideration of whether a district is a good "fit" will help ensure that you and your family don't end up in an impossible situation.
- Crafting your application materials for the specific position will begin to establish your priorities and focus as a superintendent— the district will know what they will be getting.
- Managing the interview process well helps both you and the interviewing district know what you are all about (no surprises) and helps you be certain that you can work with this particular board.
- Carving out the right language in your contract places workable understandings and parameters on your relationship with the board, and ensures you will be treated fairly should they violate these understandings.
- Staging a focused entry into the position during the first 90 days will allow you to quickly and efficiently understand the district, introduce you to all key constituents, and establish the focus of your tenure.

On the flip side, I have seen candidates who have:

- Sought the superintendency too early in their careers, and failed miserably in public.
- Applied for every superintendency that came open, ending up in a no-win situation when they weren't a good fit for the particular district in which they landed.
- Blown the interview process time and time again, never getting a superintendency despite being well-qualified.
- Agreed to standard board contract language that did not provide appropriate security for them or their family, and did not establish any expectations for the board in holding up their half of this critical relationship.

- Made critical missteps during their first few months on the job, squandered what should have been their honeymoon, and failed to get organized for success.

The guidance provided in this monograph is obviously no guarantee of getting the job, negotiating a bullet-proof contract, or succeeding in the superintendency—some communities, school boards and circumstances are just too unpredictable for that. But following these recommendations will significantly increase your chances of getting the job and enjoying lasting success.

By the way, I define success as a superintendent by two criteria:
1) being able to significantly improve student achievement for all students and close gaps in achievement between various student demographic groups, and
2) being able to manage all the other aspects of the job in a manner that allows you to stay on the job long enough to accomplish #1.

If you are reading this book, you are obviously considering your first superintendency, or are considering moving from one superintendency to another. **Being successful in getting the job and getting off to a great start won't happen by chance or by stroke of good luck. It will happen when the candidate not only has the appropriate skills and preparation for the position, but understands how to navigate the search process and properly enter the new role.**

So, as Stephen Covey would say, "Let's begin with the end in mind." This is the vision:

> *You've gotten the job of your dreams and are approaching the end of the first year in your new role. Your board has just completed your first annual evaluation. They have overwhelmed you with praise and heartfelt gratitude for your good work on behalf of children. They voted unanimously to extend your contract for three years and to award you not only a cost of living increase in salary, but a performance bonus as well. This was quite an impressive first year, and should lay the foundation for many more productive years to come.*

So how does that feel? We can't guarantee you'll experience this level of success and satisfaction, but your chances will be far greater if you can master the content of this guide.

IS THE SUPERINTENDENCY FOR YOU?

Before getting into the nuts and bolts of the superintendent search process, I'd like to talk a little "Tough Love." *Not everyone who aspires to the superintendency should become a superintendent.*

Much has been written about the qualities, skills, and characteristics necessary for someone to be successful in the superintendency—one of the most challenging jobs in America. Researchers and academics have come up with frameworks of professional standards for this role. I would like to add to those guidelines.

I have known and personally worked with well over 100 individuals across the country who have become successful superintendents. I've also known others who have failed. Some have stumbled, then regained their balance with some difficulty and went on to have successful careers. Others experienced career-ending failures.

What made the difference? Many things! Boards, finances, politics, union situations, and errors in judgment all contribute to failures. Let me offer a few of the *personal qualities* that are consistently prominent in the most successful superintendents I've known. These may not show up in any listing of professional standards stated in quite this same way, but I have witnessed them time and again...

Great Human Beings

The first quality that makes a difference is that the great superintendents are great human beings. They live their lives in a manner that engenders the respect, warmth and friendship of others. Great superintendents have great "people skills"—you cannot do this job well if you don't enjoy and love kids of all ages. In addition, they live their life in a manner that allows them to respect and like themselves.

Peak Performing Leaders

The second quality of successful superintendents is that as leaders, they continuously strive for Peak Performance. (See our monograph *In the Arena: Building the Skills for Peak Performance in Leading Schools and Systems* for a complete discussion of this.) You should not pursue a superintendency without reading that publication and developing a personal leadership plan that you revisit and update on a regular basis. Becoming a great leader is a job that is never finished—you are never "there." Defining leadership in your own terms, understanding the qualities, characteristics and skills that will get you to Peak Performance, and then appropriately managing your life are essential prerequisites to a successful superintendency. Peak Performing Leaders "have their act together" personally and professionally.

Native Intellect

The third essential quality is native intellect. "Smart" matters greatly in this role. This criteria of "smarts" for the job requires a brutally honest self-assessment. How were your SAT or ACT scores? How about your IQ and your EQ? What was your GPA during those times you truly applied yourself to your studies?

I've heard more than one not particularly bright nor skilled school district leader tell the story of watching another person "less than blessed" get the job, then convincing themselves that they, too, could be a superintendent. Unfortunately, they did—immediately placing the Peter Principle on display at the highest level of what is supposed to be every community's most critical learning organization. Their personality (or simple politics) may get them through the search process, but, unfortunately, their presence at the top of the system automatically begins to "dumb down" the entire organization. While they may be able to muddle through and survive on the job for a number of years (under an equally incompetent school board), the level of intellectual challenge in the system slips.

If you make a mistake in this and get the job when you really shouldn't, you will have a frustrating career. And you'll be doing a great disservice to the hundreds, if not thousands, of children and dedicated staff who deserve better from their leadership.

A couple of final notes on this topic—if it has not already become obvious, the attainment of a graduate degree in education is not synonymous with native intellect. And, the smartest thing that superintendents can do is surround themselves with trustworthy people who are smarter than themselves. *Unfortunately, time and time again we see the old adage play out that, "**A** people hire **A** people, and **B** people hire **C** people."*

Thick Skin

The fourth personal quality of great superintendents is thick skin. If you are someone who constantly needs approval and needs to "feel the love" of everyone, this is not the job for you. You had better be comfortable enough with who you are as a human being and as a leader to stand alone if necessary and do what is right for kids. The shrieking howls of upset constituents will be directed at you, and you will need to withstand this criticism without becoming defensive or angry, or taking it personally. Remember that those constituents may also care about kids, but they sometimes become confused in sorting out the interests of kids and the interests of adults. They may even, at times, knowingly place their own personal interests above those of children.

> *It's nuthin' personal, just business!*
> *(Career Planning Specialists)*

You can never partake in that luxury. As superintendent, you have the ultimate responsibility and moral imperative to always, always, always stand up for the interests of children— even if you must stand alone. If you are true to your value system, the slings and arrows hurled your way may draw a little blood, but will rarely lead to your career's mortality.

Political Savvy

Finally, in order to do this work well, you must develop the political savvy to navigate the often rough waters of local public leadership. The school system is typically the most emotion-laden and politically charged organization in every community. Why? Because you are dealing with the community's most precious asset—its children. And, chances are, you are also dealing with the organization that has the biggest taxpayer-funded budget and the most employees in the community.

The term "politics" automatically conjures up seedy images from our national and state political arenas. But I use the term in its most positive sense.

Political savvy is simply the capacity to anticipate the interests various constituent groups may have in the agenda or initiative you are advancing. Then, it is having the capacity to determine how to best address those interests in a manner that will move the initiative forward in the service of children. Political savvy can also be viewed as creating the support of those who wield the power of influence in the district. The position of such individuals will vary greatly from district to district—from parents to media personnel to city government officials and more.

Superintendents must accept that developing the skills—and having the *discipline* to map and address the political elements of their school community—is a critical responsibility of their job. I've heard more than one new superintendent take the stance that, "My focus is on the kids—I don't do politics." These are the superintendents who inevitably fail.

While these are obviously not the only prerequisites to becoming a successful superintendent, they are some of the most fundamental. If you measure up against these five qualities, keep reading.

If you have doubts, I'd suggest you go back to the monograph *In the Arena: Building the Skills for Peak Performance in Leading Schools and Systems*, and continue to work on your personal leadership skills before proceeding to the superintendency.

If

If you can keep your head when all about you
Are losing theirs and blaming it on you;
If you can trust yourself when all men doubt you,
But make allowance for their doubting too;
If you can wait and not be tired by waiting,
Or, being lied about, don't deal in lies,
Or, being hated, don't give way to hating,
And yet don't look too good, nor talk too wise;

If you can dream - and not make dreams your master;
If you can think - and not make thoughts your aim;
If you can meet with triumph and disaster
And treat those two imposters just the same;
If you can bear to hear the truth you've spoken
Twisted by knaves to make a trap for fools,
Or watch the things you gave your life to broken,
And stoop and build 'em up with worn out tools;

If you can make one heap of all your winnings
And risk it on one turn of pitch-and-toss,
And lose, and start again at your beginnings
And never breathe a word about your loss;
If you can force your heart and nerve and sinew
To serve your turn long after they are gone,
And so hold on when there is nothing in you
Except the Will which says to them: "Hold on";

If you can talk with crowds and keep your virtue,
Or walk with kings - nor lose the common touch;
If neither foes nor loving friends can hurt you;
If all men count with you, but none too much;
If you can fill the unforgiving minute
With sixty seconds' worth of distance run -
Yours is the Earth and everything that's in it,
And - which is more - you'll be a Man my son!

-   Rudyard Kipling

PREPARATION FOR THE SUPERINTENDENCY

How should you prepare for the superintendency? What experiences should you have under your belt? What education is required? Do you need to follow the traditional path of teacher, assistant principal, principal, and central office positions? Those are the topics covered in this chapter. Let's begin with a review of what boards are actually looking for when they begin the search process.

This mock ad printed in Education Week back in 1995 still seems to sum it up:

WANTED!
A miracle worker who can do more with less, pacify rival groups, endure chronic second-guessing; tolerate low levels of support, process large volumes of paper, and work double-shifts. He or she will have carte blanche to innovate but cannot spend much money, replace any personnel, or upset any constituency.
(Ed Week, April 12, 1995)

Most superintendent search profiles include a laundry list of qualities, skills, experiences and education that can only be described as a real life superhero. Typical criteria for superintendent candidates will usually include most or all of the following:

> - Dedication to educational excellence and the success of <u>all</u> students
> - Effective communications skills (listening, speaking and writing) with excellent interpersonal, public relations and marketing skills
> - Successful teaching and administrative experience reflecting a record of success in positions of increasing responsibility
> - Demonstrated knowledge of and experience with effective curriculum, instruction and assessment "best practices"
> - Demonstrated knowledge and experience in public school finance and fiscal management – experience with deficit elimination plans and making tough financial decisions

- Demonstrated success in human resource management including collective bargaining, contract administration and employment practices
- Demonstrated track record of direct involvement with, and knowledge of, the politics of public education at the local, state and federal levels
- An actively engaged and visible leader in the schools and the community
- Sets high standards for self and others – accepts responsibility for results
- Ability to build, direct, mentor and evaluate an effective team
- Exemplifies the highest level of personal and professional ethics, personal integrity and trust
- Sense of humor
- Proven leadership ability with skills in:
  - *Collaboration*
  - *Decision making*
  - *Systems thinking and visioning*
  - *Creative problem solving*
  - *Intelligent risk taking*
  - *Team building*
- A good understanding of facilities and operations management
- Minimum of a master's degree plus 30 credit hours in a related field of study

So, which of the above qualifications are *most* important to boards when hiring? The answer is—it depends. It will depend on the culture, the history, the current political winds in the community, and the current needs of the district. For example, if the district is facing severe financial problems, someone with a strong track record in financial management may have an edge. If the district hasn't been able to move the bar on student achievement, a candidate with a strong instructional background and proven track record in improving achievement may be preferred. Perhaps the board is simply looking for someone to come in and heal the system following a particularly difficult time. In some situations, a board may be looking for an experienced superintendent. In other situations, they may be very open to someone seeking their first superintendency.

It will also depend on the personal characteristics, strengths, and weaknesses of the prior superintendent, and how the board viewed that person. They may be looking for someone who is in every way just like the person who is leaving, or they may want the polar opposite.

Reaching consensus and coming to a conclusion on what they really want can be particularly challenging for some boards. They are ordinarily encouraged by search firms to look to the challenges and opportunities on the horizon as they contemplate the finalization of their candidate profile. They also are encouraged to consider broad school and community input on the topic as well as to review their strategic plan in detail so that they are clear about exactly what they expect to have accomplished over the next three to five years. I've seen boards be absolutely clear from day one about what they want, and I've seen others struggle through two rounds of candidate interviews before discovering their collective hearts' desire.

The best way to determine what the board is really looking for is to have a conversation with the search consultant, or whoever is leading the search, and to talk with people in your professional network who are familiar with the district. (Read more about this in the next chapter on District Fit and District Research.)

A Word about Superintendent Certification

Most states still specify credentialing requirements for school superintendents or require some form of certification. Obtaining certification usually means completing graduate courses in educational leadership and having at least three years of classroom teaching experience. (None of which, by the way, can be correlated with success as a superintendent.) There is literally a "crazy quilt" of certification requirements across the country. The credentialing requirements in one state will probably not match the requirements of another state, and licensing between states may or may not be reciprocal. This often makes it somewhat difficult for candidates from the field of education to move from state to state, and often makes it even more challenging for candidates from outside the field of education to enter the field. Specific requirements for each state can usually be obtained from that state's department of education website.

Many states will provide a provisional superintendent certificate if you have a superintendent certificate from another state. Some states will waive certification requirements for superintendents of large, urban districts in recognition of the unique challenges of those districts. At the very least, they may grant an emergency or temporary waiver and ask that the superintendent work toward meeting the certification requirements.

Check with the search consultant or the particular state department of education website to learn what might be required and what might be allowed. If you have an interest in moving to a specific state, it would be prudent to start reviewing the certification process at least a year in advance of applying for any position there.

In addition to certification issues, school accreditation organizations (such as the North Central Association) will often specify the education and experience that superintendents of districts should have for the district to maintain compliance with their accreditation standards. This is typically a Master's degree plus an additional 30 graduate credit hours in a related field, plus three years teaching experience. I have not seen any school system over the past two decades reject a candidate because they did not match the accrediting agency's standard. Nor have I seen a school system's accreditation threatened because they hired someone who did not meet these standards. The agencies will generally find a way to work with a school system to maintain their membership.

The Traditional Candidate's Path to the Superintendency

Traditional candidates are those whose professional career has been in K-12 education. A typical career ladder looks something like this:

Superintendent
Central Office
Principal
Assistant Principal
Teacher

It is usually looked upon more favorably if a candidate has spent a minimum of three to five years in each position leading to the superintendency. Having a series of one or two year stints in different districts on your resume may raise red flags about your performance, your loyalty to an organization, and your commitment to seeing your initiatives through to completion. This may have been unavoidable in your career, due to a variety of circumstances. But in that case, you should be able to satisfactorily explain your frequent moves or any gaps in employment to a search consultant.

To be competitive for the superintendency, traditional candidates generally will need to demonstrate a career path of increasingly responsible positions within K-12. For a large urban superintendency, line positions at the executive level are normally a prerequisite. These include deputy positions, "chief" positions, assistant superintendencies, or regional/area superintendencies. In a smaller, suburban, or rural district, a principalship is generally viewed as quality training ground for the superintendency. If you've taken an apparent step backwards or sideways in your career, that also raises a red flag. An example would be moving from the principalship of a large school to the principalship of a smaller school. Was the setback performance related? Is there is a valid reason for the move? Again, you should be able to explain this.

Traditional candidates who aspire to the superintendency will be most competitive with a doctoral degree, particularly in larger urban and suburban districts. A Master's degree plus additional graduate credit hours or an Education Specialist degree will usually be competitive for smaller or rural districts. The exception is that a doctorate is usually required in college/university communities, regardless of size.

Traditional candidates should seek to meet any superintendent certification requirements in their home state, as they will then face fewer hurdles meeting the requirements should they choose to relocate to another state.

The Non-Traditional Candidate's Path to the Superintendency

More and more districts, particularly urban and/or broken districts, are becoming more open to the idea of a superintendent from outside the field of education. These may be experienced leaders from the military, non-profit, private, or government sectors. Typically, non-traditional candidates will be most competitive when a district is severely dysfunctional, has a poor track record of achievement, and is generally perceived by influential constituents and the board to be in need of a major turnaround.

The non-traditional candidate's experience will generally need to include leadership of organizations with multi-million dollar budgets, large numbers of staff, and significant responsibility for management of resources. In addition, volunteer community service roles, especially those related to education and child welfare, will always be a plus factor.

Non-traditional candidates for the superintendency will generally need to have a minimum of a Master's degree to be considered.

Much has been written nationally about the phenomenon of non-traditional candidates over the past ten to fifteen years. Many traditional educators, some boards, and even some search firms have had difficulty accepting this possibility. However, that perspective is gradually changing. We are now observing increasing numbers of non-traditional candidates stepping into challenged districts and leading them to new heights.

The bottom line here is that outstanding leadership is transferrable from one arena to another. *What needs to be understood or learned at the outset is the core business of teaching and learning and the differences in organizational culture between the organizations from which they have come and that of the public school system they'll be entering.* The best non-traditional superintendents "know what they don't know" and build their leadership teams with people who have the strengths they lack.

DISTRICT FIT AND DISTRICT RESEARCH

Success as a superintendent is the result of being the right person with the right skill set in the right district at the right time. This is what we mean by "district fit."

How do you know if a district will be the right fit?

First, you will need to understand your particular leadership strengths and interests. Is your strength in instruction, finance, politics, operations, or the turn-around of failing organizations? How do those strengths match up with the needs of the district you're considering at this point in time? Do you thrive on the challenge of fixing a huge mess, or are you more interested in taking a functional district to a higher level of performance? Do you have the experience, skills, and patience to work with a dysfunctional board, or are you looking for a high-quality group of board members who know how to team with a superintendent? Is your passion with serving the children in tough urban districts or in rural communities? What size of district do you believe would be a good next step for you—500 students, 5,000 students, 25,000 students, 50,000 students, or more?

> *Don't sell what you don't have, and don't buy what you don't want.*
> *(Tim Quinn)*

If applicable, you will also need to have an understanding with your family regarding the types and locations of districts that will be acceptable to them. Are you completely mobile, or are you limited to a specific region of the country or a specific state? What quality of life must you have for your next move to be a good family fit? Where would you be willing to have your children go to school? What level of compensation must you have? Will a spouse or partner find a job that will meet his or her needs in the particular community you are considering?

Before applying for any superintendency, identify those factors most important to you. A significant beginner's mistake is to start applying for positions to see what happens. You may get well into a search and

25

interview process only to find out that this is a situation that neither you nor your family really want. Pulling out of a search process too late in the game may have a negative impact on your candidacy for future positions. Search consultants will remember, and may consider you a "shaky" bet to support a second time around. It also may resurface in future public search processes when anyone "googles" you.

Many candidates ask if they will be required to live in the district and if their children will be expected to attend the district schools. Some districts still require staff to live in the district. Some states have made this requirement illegal. Regardless, this is always a plus factor in the eyes of the board. Some boards will pay moving expenses only if the superintendent moves into the district. Making the decision to live outside the district or to have your children attend school outside the district will definitely impact your political capital.

"Choose a job you love, and you will never have to work a day in your life."
(Confucius)

I observed one candidate with some potential apply for almost every superintendency around the country that arose in districts of 20,000 or more students. In a very short period of time, he became "overexposed," and both boards and search firms were asking the question, "What is wrong with this guy? It appears that he's not sure what he wants or where he is going." They were right. Finally, a district in significant trouble (desperate for leadership) offered him the job on a split vote. Contract negotiations began, and it became apparent that his wife did not want their child to attend school in the hiring district. That bit of news, leaked to the press by one of his detractors on the board, ended negotiations and the board quickly appointed an internal candidate for the position.

Make sure you know who you are, what you want, and what will be acceptable to you and your family before you even waste your time—or anyone else's time—pursuing a position.

The "Determining District Fit" form in Appendix A is a good tool to use in thinking through these issues.

District Research

Next, you will conduct research on the district to determine what it needs and if you match those needs.

We have compiled a starter list of district research questions that you should sufficiently answer *prior* to applying for a position. (See the "District Research Starter Questions" in Appendix B.) Where do you find all this information? Here are some good sources:

- The district web site
- The search flyer for the position, including the candidate profile
- The web site of the state's department of education
- The web site of the state's teacher retirement system
- The web site of the major newspaper in the city or state.)
- National Center for Education Statistics website
- The superintendent of the local intermediate or county school district, where applicable
- Your professional network
- The web sites of important local stakeholders, including union locals, chambers of commerce, and convention and visitors bureaus
- Blogs and Facebook pages of school-related clubs and organizations and any local critics or champions of the school system
- Local demographics available from the excellent online resources of the U.S. Census Bureau

After checking those sources, any information gaps can be filled in by the search consultant or district point person leading the search. The search consultant can also discuss the candidate profile with you and tell you what is *really* important to this particular board.

You also should find out who was in the position that is vacant. How did that person do? Why did he/she leave? How long did he/she stay? What was that person's legacy? What were their strengths and blind spots? How do your personal qualifications and characteristics compare? Was the person male/female/traditional/non-traditional/white/or a person of color? How will you be viewed in the context of his/her persona and performance?

You may ask the search consultant if the outgoing superintendent is available to speak with prospective candidates. Be a little careful with this. Whether the superintendent is leaving on the best of terms or the worst of terms, he/she will likely still have influence with some of the board members. Whatever impression you leave that person with is likely to be shared.

After doing this "homework," you should be in a good position to decide if this particular district at this point in time is the right fit for you. You will know if it will be worth your time and effort to apply, and you will know that if you are selected for an interview, you'll be prepared to discuss why *you* are the best fit for them!

Finding the Positions

Where do you go to find superintendent postings? There are several places to look.

- *Education Week.* Most major superintendent searches are listed in the online edition of this weekly publication.
- The American Association of School Administrators website also lists most major superintendent vacancies.
- Monitor the websites of the state school administrators' associations and state school boards' associations in your geographical areas of interest.
- Monitor the websites of major national and regional search firms.
- Contact and meet with the search firm representatives who do business in your geographical areas of interest to let them know you are a prospective candidate and what your interests are.
- Establish a professional network of people who will let you know of opportunities as they arise in specific geographic areas of interest.

Considerations for Candidates Who Are Currently Superintendents

If you are already in a superintendency and are thinking about a move to a different district, there are several things you ought to consider:

- How long have you been in your current role? Have you been there long enough (at least 5 years) for your initiatives to take hold and to last beyond your tenure? Are your initiatives to improve student achievement showing results?

- Are you leaving your current district in a better situation than when you found it? Have you cleaned up the "messes" so your successor won't have to make unpopular decisions right off the bat?
- Is it a good time for your family to move?
- Is there still an opportunity for you to grow and learn in your current role, or do you need new challenges?
- Do your values match those of your current board members? Do new board members want the district to go in a different direction that you cannot support, as the district's leader?
- How will applying for other positions affect my relationship with my board, staff, and community?

I see superintendents make two mistakes—1) being too quick to leave a position when a little trouble comes their way, or 2) staying in a position too long. There is never a better time to leave than when you are on top and leading the parade, rather than being run out of town. But your responsibility as a leader is to stay long enough to make a significant positive and lasting difference for kids.

OVERVIEW OF THE SEARCH PROCESS

Understanding the superintendent search process is critical to your success in obtaining a superintendency. The superintendent search process is uniquely different than the process for obtaining any other job. It is, in most states, a very *public* process. And it is typically a *lengthy* process—spanning 90-120 days. I've seen some processes drag on for more than a year. Many people may be involved. Candidates need to be aware that both *substance* and *style* will be important as they go through the process.

What is the "lay of the land?"

Many things about searches seem to stay the same over time:
- Every year there are many superintendent vacancies all over the country; turnover continues at relatively high rates.
- Most boards still favor candidates with traditional K-12 backgrounds.
- Almost all unions still favor traditional candidates.
- Race and gender are always factors in the process.
- Any public event or electronic posting from your past can and will be "googled."

But some things are changing:
- In larger districts, business communities are becoming increasingly involved in superintendent search processes.

> *Only those who dare to fail greatly can ever achieve greatly.*
> *(Robert F. Kennedy)*

- As public education moves from an "entitlement" culture to a "performance" culture with an increasing emphasis on accountability, the opportunities increase for nontraditional candidates.
- More states are granting certification waivers for nontraditional candidates, particularly for challenged districts.
- There are increasing opportunities for female superintendent candidates.
- There are increased local political turf battles impacting the search process.

Phases of the Search Process

Regardless of size or type of district, there are four general phases of a superintendent search process:
1. The Preparation Phase
2. The Recruitment and Application Phase
3. The Interview Phase
4. The Closing Phase

During each phase, both the board (and its search firm) and the candidates have several tasks to complete. In this section, I'll provide an overview of each phase from both the board's and the candidate's perspectives. Specific advice on working with a search consultant, handling the interview, and negotiating the superintendent's contract will be covered in more depth in later chapters.

The Preparation Phase

Board Tasks

Before seeking candidates, the board will do the following, usually with the assistance of a search firm and its professional staff:
- Determine the specific search process that will be followed
- Determine the search timeline; commit to specific dates for key benchmarks in the process
- Develop the candidate profile—generally with input from the school community either through public forums, focus groups, or online input
- Determine the compensation range for the position, and what types of backgrounds would qualify for the bottom and the top of the range
- Determine the appropriate roles during the search of:
  - The board members
  - The board officers or search committee
  - The search firm, if used
  - Citizen and staff groups

Sometimes boards will attempt to conduct their own search, usually in an attempt to save money. When they do, it can be an opportunity for those who are not likely to get through the scrutiny of a professional search firm. Boards who attempt to do their own searches (unless they are comprised of professionals who have lots of spare time) may end up reaching out to someone with a little more time and expertise for help. Sometimes this is the superintendent of a regional education agency, a county superintendent, or a former superintendent living in the area.

Candidates applying for positions being coordinated by a board without the assistance of a professional firm should be cautious. This is not intended to be a criticism of boards or their good intentions, but simply a sharing of our observations over the years of board-coordinated searches:

- Information provided about the position, district and timeline may be sketchy
- The confidentiality of candidates (as allowed by pertinent state laws) is more likely to be breached
- Search protocols and timelines will generally be less well-managed than if a professional search firm is involved; the search process may break down in the final stages
- Absent the recruitment efforts of a professional firm, the overall candidate pool is likely to be more shallow
- The search is more likely to be wired for an internal candidate
- Reaching consensus on the top candidate may be extremely difficult

Candidate Tasks

In preparation for entering a superintendent search, you must also do your homework.

- Determine your needs and interests
- Do your research on the district and determine if there is a "fit" with this district (refer to prior chapter)
- Obtain the position profile, search process, and time line; this will normally be on the district's web site and/or the search consultant's web site
- Talk to the search consultant or person leading the search regarding your background, the process to be followed, roles of all the players during the process, how long names of candidates will be held in confidence, at what step in the process names will be released publicly, and any unique certification issues in the particular state

The Recruitment and Application Phase

Board Tasks

The search is now under way. There are several activities that either the board or the search consultant will be executing during this phase of the process:
- Advertising in print and/or online posting sites
- Recruiting candidates
- Receiving applications
- Managing media and public interest
- Screening applications
- Checking references
- Identifying the candidates to be interviewed

The laws of each state will determine how confidential the applications can be at this point. In some states, all applications become public information immediately upon receipt. In some states, districts are able to keep names of applicants final until public interviews are held. In others, candidates can be interviewed privately and only the finalist announced publicly. Regardless of state law, individual boards may decide to make the process more public than required if there is precedent in the district to do so or there is strong pressure from the public and the media. Also, be aware that the media may obtain (and make public) the names of candidates after the search is completed.

Candidate Tasks

You have a few tasks during the implementation phase, as well.

> *It is fatal to enter any war without the will to win it.*
> *(Douglas McArthur)*

- Discuss your intentions with your current supervisor or employer at the appropriate time (prior to your candidacy becoming public.) There is nothing worse than having them learn of your candidacy from another source. If you are currently a superintendent, you may be able to have a confidential conversation with your board chair about this. Based upon that discussion, you may decide to have the conversation with your entire board. You may defer this second step until after you are invited to interview.
- Prepare your cover letter, resume, and any other paper required and have it all reviewed by someone you trust (other than your

spouse—they tend to have blind spots when it comes to their partner's efforts.) This person should understand the education field and be able to provide unbiased feedback on how you are presenting yourself.

- In many searches these days, submission of application materials occurs entirely online. You still need to have someone review and proofread what you plan to submit, so there are no errors.

- Make sure that contact information for your references is current and that your references are informed of your candidacy. You might talk with them about what strengths you hope they could attest to on your behalf.

- Be sure to follow the application instructions. If they say not to contact board members, don't contact board members. If they don't ask for letters of reference or portfolio materials, don't include them.

- Monitor the local media to understand current events in the community and the district, and pursue follow-up questions based on what you read.

- Talk to the search consultant, if necessary, to explain any "blips" in your history. Now is the time to have the conversation with them about that DUI you had when you were 20, or your rather public divorce five years ago, or your untimely departure from a previous position. You will need to be able to explain any potentially negative thing that may be found in the public record or on the internet. The search consultant needs to hear this information from you if they are going to help the board put this "blip" in the proper context of your stellar career. Do not let the search firm or the board be surprised by one of these events by reading about it in the local paper or hearing it from a citizen who googled you thoroughly.

- Visit the district to get a better feel for it. At this point, you should be visiting the district and community as a potential resident— rather than as a superintendent candidate. Now is the time for your family to decide if this is some place they might like to live. Don't wait until after you've been offered the job!

Interview Phase

Board Tasks

Often, the search consultant will conduct preliminary interviews with strong candidates, especially if they don't know you. These interviews are done either in person or by phone. Their goal is to narrow the field of candidates to the top five or six to be taken to the board. They want to make sure the candidates they take will interview well, be a good fit for the district, and (at a minimum) not be an embarrassment to them or to the board in the process.

The next step is to have the first interview with the board. These are generally standard interviews, approximately 90 minutes each, and consistent for each candidate. (The interview process is covered in more depth in the following chapter.) Generally, the board will interview four to six candidates.

After first interviews are completed, the board will narrow the field and typically invite two or three candidates back for an in-depth second interview. These are normally all-day affairs and, in many cases, involve a series of meetings with various constituent groups and/or open public forums. The day usually ends with an interview with the board. This interview will be more customized for each candidate than the first interview was, allowing the board to "fill in any gaps" they may have in their knowledge of you.

Some boards may then opt to do a visitation to the district or place of employment of their finalist(s). This usually lasts from 4 – 6 hours. They will want to meet with several groups of people to talk with them personally about your leadership style and strengths. This topic is also covered in more depth in the next chapter.

Candidate Tasks

You will be busy during this phase of the process. Don't think that just because you are "good on your feet" you can naturally ace this part of the test. Be prepared!

- Prepare by doing your research on the district—know more about the district than the board does. Practice by having a colleague walk you through a mock interview.

- Develop "killer" opening and closing statements. Make a strong first impression and a memorable last impression. (See the chapter on interviewing for more on this topic.)
- Understand how and when their search process will conclude, so you can plan for this time line.
- Have your professional photo ready or available to the media electronically—don't let the community's first snapshot of you be taken by a cub reporter with a cheap digital camera, with you standing in front of a messy bulletin board. Prepare a brief bio.
- Dress for success—have your interview clothes ready.
- Be prepared for anything! At this point, when the board and the public get involved, anything can happen. Be mentally ready for anything that might get thrown at you—off-the-wall questions, odd interview formats, etc. While I haven't been party to such an occasion, I've heard accounts of boards going "off script" and asking illegal questions or putting candidates in impromptu situations such as asking them to make a presentation on a particular topic. Be mentally prepared for anything.
- Plan for an outstanding site visit to your district, if applicable.

Closing Phase

Board Tasks

Three main steps occur in this phase:
- Offer and acceptance of the position
- Public announcements and media coverage of your appointment
- Completion of contract negotiation

Candidate Tasks

At the point your appointment is announced, you will need to have public statements prepared for both your old and new employers and the respective communities.

Regarding contract negotiation, you should:
- Know your needs; develop realistic expectations of what you can reasonably obtain in this position and in your first contract
- Know the closing process and roles of the players in the process
- Secure the prior superintendent's contract

- Ask the state superintendent's association for a model contract for that state
- Retain an attorney if the district will be using one, to negotiate your contract. If the district is not using an attorney, retain one anyway to provide, at minimum, behind the scenes review before signing.

Time is of great importance at this stage. You do not want the board to lose interest in you and move on.

Refer to the subsequent chapter on Superintendent Contract Negotiations for more details on this topic.

WORKING WITH THE SEARCH FIRM

Most superintendent searches today are coordinated by a professional search firm—either an independent, private firm or one sponsored by a state school board association or some other education-related organization. It is important for candidates to understand the protocols and "etiquette" for working with search consultants.

The Search Firm Relationship

Keep in mind that a significant majority of those involved in the search business are former (and most often retired) school superintendents. They come to the process with their own set of values, judgments, and biases about what makes a good school superintendent. Do some research in advance on the specific individual handling the search. Find out where they have been, what they have done, and what they might be most proud of during their careers. Getting to know them through the process is always a good idea as long as it is not *over*done to the extent that the candidate is perceived as being inauthentic, "needy," or "high maintenance." In some cases, you may have an opportunity to meet with the search consultant either prior to or following formal submission of application. In other instances, the opportunity to get to know them will be through phone or email exchanges. Remember that every communication you have with them is part of the interview and selection process, so take these contacts seriously and always be at your professional best.

Always remember, too, that *the search consultant is working for the board*, and is not necessarily your friend. Any search consultant worth their salt can be expected to treat candidates with respect and do everything in their power to help candidates negotiate the process successfully—but they still are working for the board. They also are trying to recruit a strong candidate pool to present to the board. You can be flattered if they reach out to you to be a candidate, but remember that managing your professional career path is not their primary interest here. Do not feel compelled to apply for a position if it doesn't feel like the right fit or the right time for you to make a move. There will be other opportunities when you are ready.

As a candidate, just remember that the responsibility for establishing and maintaining a relationship with the consultant is one you should assume since you have the most to lose if it does not go well. Extend your best professional self to them whether you win the job or not. For the vast majority of candidates, there will always be another search sometime in the future. If you blow your relationship with the search firm, they won't forget—and they are likely to share their observations with their peers.

Prior to Formal Application

The search firm representative will have spent time in the community with the board, and probably more extensive time with the board chair. They should have a good grasp of the position and what the board is looking for at this particular point in the district's history. Oftentimes, the candidate profile tells only part of the story of the board's ideal candidate. It is fair game to ask the search consultant any questions unanswered by the postings or electronic search flyers. Questions also may pertain to confidentiality of the process, timing of calls to references, the search calendar, composition, stability and tenure of the board, and compensation range.

Make sure that you follow the directions provided by the firm. If they tell you not to contact board members, don't contact board members. If they tell you they want five letters of reference, provide them with five letters of reference. If they tell you that they simply want references and contact information, that's what you provide. Don't send them stacks of other materials unless they tell you they want to see it. Generally, large portfolios are not warranted nor appreciated.

As noted earlier, this is the right time to speak with the search firm representative about any personal "blips" in your personal or professional track record. They need to know if you have had a DUI, been fired from a position, resigned under threat of dismissal, or have anything else in your past that is going to show up when they, community education groupies or an investigative reporter make calls or get on the internet to "check you out." The worst thing you can do is to let your search firm rep be surprised by anything of this sort. If they hear it from you in advance, they will likely respect your honesty and, if at all possible, help you frame the situation in an appropriate light for the board and the general public. The only thing worse than having the search firm be surprised by something in your past is having the board and community surprised after you have been publicly named as a finalist. The latter will definitely destroy your candidacy and create media reports that will not be helpful in future job searches.

One search executive pointed out that, clearly, a great superintendent is not always going to be the most popular person in a district. Moving schools and districts from Point A to a much-improved Point B takes time, energy, and tough decisions. There are going to be challenges, unfavorable headlines, and both constructive and destructive criticism heaped upon the superintendent. Many candidates struggle with this, and try to downplay or ignore these "blips," which can create problems during the search process. It is much better for candidates to be open, honest, and clear in addressing these situations, with both the search firm and the board.

During the Interview Phase

If you are under serious consideration and the search firm rep has not already met you in person, they may want to have an extended phone conversation with you before presenting candidates to the board. When this happens, take it seriously and treat it like your initial interview. If you get a cold call to do this, it is fair to ask if you can speak with them at a time of mutual convenience. Then make sure:

- You have reviewed your homework on the system
- You can tell your story of accomplishment in the context of this district's needs
- They know you definitely are interested in this opportunity
- You are prepared with any final questions you have before they take your name to the board.

Maintain communication with your search firm representative during the interview process. If they are doing their job, they will have a feel for the pulse of the board and the ebb and flow of the interviews. They may offer advice and feedback between rounds of interviews, and you should seriously consider what they have to say.

Protocols for Withdrawing

Keep in mind that the search firm will have invested a good deal of time in getting you and the board to this point. There is nothing more frustrating to a search firm representative than having candidates decide to withdraw after they have been recommended to the board for interview. This creates scheduling problems, creates more work, and hurts their credibility by making it look like they haven't done their homework. Actually, there is one thing that makes them more upset than this—having a candidate selected as the superintendent and then backing out. This puts them in a situation where they have to start the search all over again—usually for no additional fee. At each step along the way, they are going to be thinking of you, and not fondly.

That doesn't mean that you can't get out of the process once you get in. You can get out with no harm and without antagonizing your search firm rep before candidates are presented to the board. We have seen candidates do this a number of times after submitting their application, then completing their research for interview prep. If you don't think it is a fit, don't force it and don't lead the search firm on.

The other point in the search process when it is considered fair game to get out is following the first interview with the board. The firm will have coached the board to understand that you will be interviewing them as well as them interviewing you. If the board doesn't "show well," and you decide that you don't want to be professionally married to this group of people for the next phase of your career, bow out of the process at this stage. Make sure that the search firm rep is the first one to know immediately after you decide. **Don't go to the second round of interviews without being certain you want the job.**

Often times we see sitting superintendents go through this process (particularly if it's a public process) with a great deal of anxiety. They're concerned about the reaction from their board, their community, and their staff back home and want to avoid—at all costs—coming in second or third in a very public way. They are concerned that it might make the folks at home begin to question not only their loyalty, but what the other district learned that caused them to reject "their" superintendent.

Sitting superintendents will often be seen bowing out of the process at the point they don't believe they have a good chance of being the final candidate, publicly renewing their commitment to their current district. Sometimes this is done prematurely, and sometimes it is done too late. Your best source of information on how the process is going for you is the search consultant. Keep them apprised of your thoughts and concerns, and in the vast majority of cases, they can let you know if things have turned and that it's time for a graceful exit from the process.

After Selection

If you end up getting the job, thank the search firm representative profusely and seek their advice as you proceed with your entry. Again, they will have worked with the board and will know the hot button issues, concerns, and needs. Plus, there is no greater compliment to a retired superintendent than to be asked for advice.

If you don't get the job, thank the search firm representative profusely for their help in the process. It is fair to ask for their feedback on your candidacy and how you can improve in future searches. They won't forget how you handle a loss.

APPLICATIONS AND RESUMES

The paper you submit won't get you the job, but it can get you in the door. If not done well, your application materials can quickly place your candidacy in the "circular file." We have seen a few people with horrible resumes get the job. But in those instances, some other unique political factors were at play.

We've all obtained advice on resume development over the course of our careers, some of it conflicting. College placement offices have one idea of how the information should be presented. Private resume firms and outplacement services may have another. Your mentors and peers will have others. Some like a chronological presentation of experience; some prefer a functional presentation. Some suggest a graphically designed slick package; others prefer a simple format. When applying for many positions today, you may find that the entire application is online and you will be required to follow the format of the respective board or search firm.

The advice provided in this section is based upon years of experience in the superintendent search business, years of successful placement of superintendent candidates in all types of districts, and conversations with leading search professionals across the country. I've observed countless examples of what **not** to submit when seeking a superintendency.

In addition to any district or search firm application form, there are two key written components when applying for the superintendency—the cover letter and the resume. In preparing both of these, keep the initial reader in mind. This person is likely to be a search consultant, faced with reviewing a stack of applications for the position. Their initial goal is to cull the number of applications down to about a dozen to be given more serious review. At this phase, they are looking for reasons to *exclude* you – don't give them a good or an easy reason.

Once you have made it past the search consultant screening, your paper will next be reviewed by board members. Let them get to know you and make your first impression a positive one. Keep in mind that board members are usually non-educators who will not understand, nor appreciate, a lot of educational jargon or acronyms. Grammatical errors and misspellings, especially by someone aspiring to lead their educational system, usually terminates a candidacy.

Application Forms

You will need to complete either a district application form or a form developed by the specific search firm, either in hard copy or online. Obviously, be sure that everything you put on the form is true and complete. The form is where you will be asked questions about your reasons for leaving prior positions, prior convictions, beginning and ending compensation, etc. Don't leave blanks. Don't fudge information. If you need to add explanations to provide a complete picture, do so. If anything on this form is later found to be incorrect or misleading, it can be cause for dismissal. In some instances you'll be asked to provide information on the application form that is already included in your resume—include it again anyway. Do not say, "See resume."

Cover Letters

The purpose of the cover letter is to introduce yourself and raise interest in your candidacy. You will have about 30-60 seconds to capture the attention of the reader, so the letter should be **no more than two pages** long. Here are some simple guidelines:

- Don't use letterhead from your current employer!! (very tacky—and, yes, we've seen it done repeatedly)
- Determine to whom the letter should be addressed, the correct spelling, salutation and title
- Customize the letter based upon your research on the district; there is nothing worse than a standard, generic application letter that you use to apply for several positions—it shows
- Explain why you really want this position and how your track record fits the district's needs as outlined in the candidate profile
- Create a mental image of you—share your passion and your vision; the resume speaks to the left brain, but your cover letter should speak to the right brain
- Be clear about who you are and what you will bring to the system
- Communicate clearly and concisely in a conversational, rather than stilted, manner
- Include any special instructions regarding confidentiality and how to best contact you
- You may request confidentiality up to a certain point in the process

In lieu of a cover letter, some electronic application processes may ask you to complete an essay responding to the question, "Why do you want this position?" This is where you would provide the above information.

Because the cover letter should be uniquely personalized, I hesitate to provide a model. It needs to be you speaking. The sample shown in Appendix C is a good example of a letter from a specific candidate for a specific position.

Resumes

As the old saying goes, "You never get a second chance to make a first impression." Make it count! If applying with a hard copy resume, my general advice for the superintendency is:

> *"You can't always judge a book by its cover, but it's still the first thing you see."*
> *(Anonymous)*

- Customize to the specific job—spotlight accomplishments that relate to this district's needs
- Use 8-1/2 x 11 white or off-white, high quality paper, of a slightly heavier weight than standard copy paper. Your resume will get scanned and copied multiple times, so special sizes, bright colors, folded, or bound papers will not be presented well. Make it easy for the search consultant to handle.
- Keep it to 3-5 pages maximum; this is a superintendent application, not a *curriculum vitae*
- At this point, don't include photographs of yourself—no matter how good looking you think you are
- Use an 11 or 12 point, easily readable, common font (most of the people who will be reading your materials wear reading glasses)
- Don't crowd your information—it should be easy to visually scan your resume

Following are the standard sections of a resume, and advice on each. A sample resume template is included in Appendix D. (If you are required to apply online rather than with a hard copy resume, many of these same guidelines will apply when presenting your information.)

Header and Contact Information

Put your name up there in bigger, bold font. Don't be shy. You want them to remember you.

Include all of your contact information—preferred mailing address and telephone numbers, including cell phone number. Be sure to use your *non-work* email address. If you are currently employed, you will not want emails related to job searches coming to your office. You don't want to run the risk of staff seeing this communication. In addition, if you are employed in the public sector, these emails are public information.

Make it easy for the search consultant to contact you at any time of the day or night. Many search processes will play out in the evening or over weekends, and become more unpredictable in their later stages.

This is a good time to check the voice mail greeting on your phones. Be sure they project professionalism. This isn't the time to have a cute family message for callers.

Objective

I hate this section. Don't include it. At best, statements of objective are wasted space. At worst, they are out of date and totally unrelated to the job the person is applying for. Everyone assumes your objective is to get this superintendency. What you may opt for instead is a brief profile or summary of your achievements, strengths, skills, and leadership characteristics. Here is where you would describe yourself "in a nutshell."

Education

The first key criteria in screening superintendent candidates is education: Does this candidate have at least a Master's degree, or not? So go ahead and make it easy for the search consultant—put this section right near the beginning. Don't make them hunt for it.

Advice for presenting your educational background includes:
- Organize the information by degree, most recent first
- Show the degree, the major, the university, and honors received—in that order. The degree you have is the most important piece of information here, not the college. (The exception is if you attended a highly prestigious university, such as Harvard, Yale, or The University of Michigan.)
- Include the date the degree was attained. If your most recent degree is over 10 years old, provide evidence of recent

professional development activities in a later section of your resume.

- Don't include your GPA unless it was 3.9 or above; they will get your official transcripts later. You can include any academic honors here.
- Include work toward a graduate degree, stating when the degree is anticipated
- Never, ever imply that you have a degree if it has not yet been awarded
- You may include certifications in this section if the position you are applying for requires certification, or you may insert a separate section later in the resume

Professional Experience

This is the section of the resume most educators fail. The reason they fail is that they focus on *responsibilities* and *process activities* rather than on *outcomes* and *accomplishments*.

Guidelines for presenting your experience:
- List employment in reverse chronological order, most recent first
- Account for all years since college
- State the position, the employer, city, state, and years of employment (you don't need to include the specific months)
- Include a brief statement explaining the scope of responsibility and characteristics of the organization, such as number and demographics of students, size of budget managed, number of schools, number of staff supervised
- Focus on responsibilities that may not be common to the position; in other words, the job of a principal needs little explanation. But if you served as chair of the district-wide planning team while you were principal, mention that.
- If you had part-time work in addition to your regular positions, such as serving as adjunct faculty at a local university, put that in a separate section (e.g. Additional Professional Experiences) so that it doesn't get confusing to the reader trying to track your dates of employment.

Under each of your most recent positions, bullet your major accomplishments. Tell what you did and what the results were. Use numbers where possible. Which of the following is a more powerful statement?

"Facilitated a district-wide reading committee"
or
"Established a new reading program that resulted in an increase in proficiency from 35% to 75% over 4 years"

Tips for bulleting your accomplishments:
- Avoid using the word "I"
- Use strong action verbs such as achieved, initiated, led, transformed. Most educators don't like to take personal credit for group accomplishments and often use the word "facilitated." You should use this inclusive language when you *interview and talk* to groups, but not necessarily in your resume.
- Be selective—include no more than 7 bullets under each job. Highlight what is most important and related to the particular job you are applying for. Don't drag out the whole laundry list and bore the reader or confuse them about what is most important in the context of their needs.
- Avoid unexplained acronyms and educational jargon—assume that lay board members reading your resume will not understand "education-ese."
- After your most recent 3 or 4 jobs, simply list your title, organization, location, and years of service. Accomplishment bullets are not needed unless you did something incredibly spectacular related to this position's needs and/or that put you on the map professionally.

> **"The product you are selling is yourself. Give them reasons to buy."**
> *(Carole Martin)*

Functional Experience Presentation

Non-traditional candidates may want to include a functional presentation of their experience. This means presenting your experience by category or function, rather than by position and dates held. This can help the reader draw connections between your prior non-education experience and the K-12 world.

If this is done, the functional presentation should also be followed by a chronological presentation of your positions and dates. The reader will want to track your career progression and be assured that there are no employment gaps or backward steps.

In the functional presentation, think of what this district is looking for and organize or present your information with that in mind. Be sure to use every day, understandable language—no industry buzz-words common only to your prior profession. Of special interest will be your experience with:

- Leadership – leading large, complex organizations in a highly diverse setting
- Improving results – measurable success of organizations under your leadership, planning and organizational skills, accountability for results
- Financial management – large, multi-million dollar budget responsibility
- Labor relations – experience with labor unions
- Instruction – experience with teaching, curriculum, instructional leadership
- Public relations – effective communication, collaborative leadership, and coalition-building with state, community, media, and other pertinent political forces
- Personnel management – selecting, managing, and evaluating staff

Alternatively, a Summary section may be used at the beginning of the resume, describing your related leadership strengths.

Professional/Community Activities, Honors, Presentations, Publications

These sections are for the "plus factors" that may differentiate you from the pack. For the superintendency, boards will be looking for candidates who have been active in the community. Leadership roles in professional associations and any honors and awards are value-added inclusions.

A word of caution—if you have an extensive list of presentations, entitle the section "Selected Presentations" and include no more than 8-10 of the most relevant and most significant. These would be those presentations on a state or national stage and most related to the superintendency. Again, this is a resume for the superintendency, not a *Curriculum Vitae*. (Save that for when you retire and want to join a college or university faculty.) Plus, if it appears that you are constantly out speaking at conferences, board members will wonder if you'll have the time to manage their district.

Personal data, interests, and hobbies are generally not included on a professional resume unless there is something in your past that could be of unique interest to this particular board. In general, the smaller the school district, the more they are interested in what you do during your spare time.

I once worked with a candidate who worked every summer during his college days at a Florida theme park. His actual position title was "Alligator Wrestler." Can't you just picture what that would have entailed? He told me that including that single line on his resume had gotten him an interview for almost every position for which he had ever applied. He said he had always received at least one question and a good dose of comic relief out of it in each interview.

While that may have served him well as a candidate in small, rural districts, it's just as likely to be a candidacy killer in a wealthy suburban district. Bottom line—use some common sense and good judgment based on the context of the specific position.

References

You will be asked to provide professional references. (Your resume doesn't need to say "references provided upon request"—of course they will.) Provide what is requested, but generally you'll be asked to include four to six references. It is fair to ask the search consultant not to contact references until they have talked with you about where you stand in the process after all applications have been received. Some advice:

- Be sure the contact information is current, complete and correct. The search consultant may eliminate you as a candidate rather than go on a hunting expedition to track down your references.
- Let your references know the position you are applying for, that they have been listed as a reference, and they should expect a call. As noted earlier, you might also discuss with each the particular strengths to which they can attest.
- Make sure your references are people you know will be 100% supportive of your candidacy.
- It always raises a red flag if you do not include your current supervisor as a reference. If that is the case, make sure the search consultant understands why.
- You may add or delete specific references based upon the composition of the hiring board. For example, if the board

52

includes a prominent member of the religious community or the local business community, you may want to include similar persons in your references.

Delivery

In general, follow the specific instructions provided by the search consultant. If sending a hard copy, it's best to send the materials requested in via USPS Express Mail, FedEx, or other tracked delivery service. Do not send them through the mail system of your current employer.

We generally suggest that the closer to the deadline you apply, the better, unless specifically requested to do so earlier by the search consultant. Make your candidacy a pleasant surprise to the person responsible for recommending quality people to the board. It also provides less opportunity for your candidacy to become public earlier than necessary in those states where candidate applications are considered public information.

THE SUPERINTENDENT INTERVIEW PROCESS

You can get the job without a great resume, but not without a great interview.

The superintendent interview process is played out in several steps, usually lasting about a month in duration. There will generally be:
- An initial or preliminary interview with the search consultant
- The first interview with the board
- A second interview with the board and, in many cases, school community groups
- A site visitation to your current place of employment if deemed relevant

In some states, the interview process can be confidential, with candidate interviews conducted "behind closed doors." Some states allow complete confidentiality until the final candidate is named. Others may keep all applications confidential except for final interviews conducted in public.

Preliminary Interview with Search Consultant

Prior to taking candidates to the board, many search consultants will conduct a preliminary interview with top candidates, particularly if they don't know you. This interview is either in person or via telephone. They want to know if you will present yourself well and interview well with the board. They'll also want to ask questions that your paperwork doesn't answer to determine how good a fit you'll be for this particular position.

Generally, here is what they will want to discuss with you:
- Your career experience
- Your competencies as related to the criteria for the position
- Your record of accomplishments and the impact of those accomplishments
- Whether you would be a good fit for this district
- Your references—who they are and how they know you
- Your compensation needs
- Any personal issues or needs for confidentiality you may have

- Explanation of any "skeletons" in your closet that may emerge into public view during the search process
- Whether you are an applicant for other positions, and your status in those search processes

And, generally, they'll want to check out your overall presence. If this is an in-person interview, make sure you dress for the occasion—just like you would for your interview with the board.

You should also be prepared to ask them questions, if you haven't been able to find the answers through your district research:

> *"Instead of the Inquisition, think of a job interview as a first date: You're both trying to figure out if there's a match."*
> *(Marty Nemko)*

- Why is the incumbent leaving?
- What is missing from the published profile of the ideal candidate?
- What major challenges will the new superintendent be facing in this district at this time?
- What can you tell me about the board members, board relationships, their tenures, and their terms of office?
- What is the search and selection process and time line?
- How confidential will the process be? At what point will candidates' names be made public?
- Will there be any internal candidates?
- What will the general compensation range be?
- What feedback can you give me on my qualifications and fit at this point in time?

If the preliminary interview is being conducted by phone, you can treat this like an open-book test. Use a crib sheet—have a "script" addressing likely questions. List five reasons why hiring you would be a tremendous benefit to the district and be sure these get covered during the interview. Because 90% of human communication is nonverbal, you'll need to overcome this built-in problem. Stand up—it changes your breathing and tone of voice, and can make you sound more alert and confident.

Your First Interview with the Board

It's show time! Your knowledge, experience, application, resume, and references got you this far. From this point forward, it's all about how well you connect with people and present your knowledge and skills.

Preparation for the Interview

As noted earlier, don't rely on your ability to think on your feet—that generally doesn't work in this situation. You must be completely prepared, or it will show.

- Review your research on the district and read any materials they send. You should know more about them and the district than they know about themselves.
- Know the backgrounds of board members. What are their respective occupations? What are their interests? Be able to address each board member by name and appropriate title.
- Review recent media reports about the district. Know what their current issues and concerns are so you don't accidentally step on any land mines.
- Make contacts with your network. What do they know about the district?
- Attend superintendent interviews in another district (or watch online videos of superintendent interviews) to see what happens, what is effective, and what isn't.
- Conduct an advance visit to the district if you need to. However, if you do this after you are an announced candidate, be very thoughtful and intentional about how you do it. Every contact you have with people will be scrutinized. Nothing is casual at this point. Assume that anything observed or heard will make it back to the board.
- Practice answering potential interview questions using the questions in Appendix E. Have a trusted associate run you through a mock interview. This should be someone who has observed superintendent interviews (and preferably has been through several personally) and who can give you constructive comments and feedback on your answers.
- Develop questions you will ask the board. For the first interview, these should be "softball" questions that put them in touch with their vision for the district and their feelings for kids. Don't try to

stump them or ask technical questions that would be difficult for them to respond to without additional research.

- Have professional photos ready to provide to district communications staff and local reporters electronically. You want your first impression to be a good one. Don't let the community's first view of you be a mug shot taken by a cub reporter. (You know—the one with your mouth open and your hair out of place.) In addition, prepare a very brief bio—one that you'd be happy to read in the local media.

Dressing for Success—Our Advice

What does dressing for success mean in this day and age? Men should obviously wear a dark business suit. The traditional dark suit, blue shirt, and red tie are never out of style in this situation.

Our advice to women is to wear whatever makes you feel powerful and comfortable. It's OK to wear a professional-looking pantsuit, a regular suit, or a skirt and jacket. Avoid flowery prints or pastel colors—deeper solids are "power" colors. You should have some idea through your research as to whether or not the district is conservative and traditional. Avoid flashy or clunky jewelry that will distract from you and what you have to say. Don't drag along a suitcase-sized purse or wear impractical shoes, as you may be taking a walking tour of the district. Keep the Rolex and big diamonds at home. Expensive jewelry (on women and men) can be a put-off to some trustees.

Some small grooming tips—both men and women should have a fresh haircut in a personally appropriate style. If you haven't had your teeth whitened recently, do it now. Polish your shoes. Get a good night's sleep before the interview. And be in the best physical condition of your life— vitality affects your presence. (Plus, you will need this strength and stamina if you get the job!)

Thoughts about Presence

When interviewing for the superintendency, your overall *presence* will be important. Do you seem like a leader? Presence is that intangible *"it"* factor that can be defined as how you carry yourself, your bearing, your self-assurance and confidence. It is hard to define, but you know it when you see it. People 6'4" tall can have great presence, as well as people who are 5'2". Various factors go into presence:

- Your dress and style
- Your physical condition
- Your voice
- Your mastery of issues
- Your sincerity
- Your passion
- Your confidence
- Your smile and sense of humor
- Your connection with people

Be aware of the presence you project. Will it serve you well in the context of this situation?

Board Interview Formats

The format of the first interview will vary from district to district.

- If the law allows, the interviews may be in closed session rather than in public. If in public, count on the media being present.
- The interviews may be videotaped and broadcast online.
- The interviews may be with the full board, a sub-group of the board, or others in addition to the board. Some boards may invite students or a "search committee," including staff and community representatives, to sit in on first interviews.
- The room setup will vary by district. You may be on a stage. You may be facing the board with your back to the audience. You may be sitting at a conference table or standing at a podium.
- At this point, the public may or may not be allowed to ask you questions or comment about you.
- There will generally be 25-30 questions asked of each candidate, usually scheduled in ninety minute or two-hour blocks. This includes time for your questions of the board.

Bottom line—be mentally prepared for anything!

Candidates often ask if they should bring their spouse or partner to the interview. My answer is—only if they are an asset. We've seen candidates win and lose jobs based upon what the spouse brought to the equation. Perhaps a trusted colleague who knows your partner could give you feedback on this. It isn't necessarily expected and can easily turn out to be either a plus factor or a liability to your candidacy. Do not take your spouse without adequately coaching and preparing them for the experience. Oftentimes, the spouse is not expected at the first interview, but if you are invited back for a second interview, the spouse may very well be invited for a parallel visitation day in the district. Their attendance is often encouraged at this stage, to be sure they are "on board" if the job is offered.

Two quick examples come to mind where leading candidates have lost the job due to their spouses. The first was in an upscale suburb when the leading candidate brought his wife to the second interview. The actual interview was preceded by a community reception and then dinner with the board. The candidate's wife was well-educated, but obviously nervous and could not stop talking. During both the public reception and the board dinner she completely dominated each and every conversation—she didn't ask a single question and didn't pause to take a breath. By the time the dinner was over, the board was frustrated and exhausted. They had not had an opportunity for any informal conversation with the candidate, and they had each concluded independently that they didn't want to deal with the "first lady" this candidate would bring to the district. Obviously, they selected the other candidate.

The second example was in a rural district that was ready to hire their first female superintendent. She had "wowed" them in the first interview and, going into the second interview, it was her job to lose. She entered the interview room first and was working the crowd with grace and aplomb, when "He" showed up. Blue jeans, T-shirt, and a biker's helmet under his arm—he had obviously ridden in on his own. After greeting his wife, the prospective "first gentleman" took a seat in the first row and placed his helmet on the seat next to him. Hands behind his head and T-shirt riding up over his expansive belly, he settled in to watch his better half go for the job of her dreams. She had a great interview, but the board was distracted by what they <u>didn't</u> want as an adjunct member of their team—a colorfully tattooed and unkempt significant other representing them in the community. He was probably a great guy and was obviously supportive of his wife. But, unfortunately, the candidate's abiding love of her partner completely clouded her professional judgment – and wrecked her chances of getting the job.

Bottom line—if you have a spouse, and they are invited to the interview, they are being evaluated also. Prepare them, leave them at home, or find a community where they, too, will either be a good fit or considered non-essential to your role in the community.

The same advice goes for bringing school-age children to the interview. Nothing can be a greater asset to a candidate than adorable, well-behaved children (and the increased revenue they may bring to the district!) But, no matter how well-behaved, you probably do not want your young children sitting in on a 90-minute interview. One effective option we've observed is to have the spouse bring the children in just prior to the interview, to be introduced, but then exit prior to the start of the formal interview.

Acing the Interview

There are three parts to every interview:
- The first ten minutes
- The last ten minutes
- The rest of the interview

The First Ten Minutes

Interviewers often make a decision about you in the first 5-10 minutes of the interview. It begins when you walk in the room, so you need to make a great first impression. Here are some tips to remember:
- Interpersonal skills are more important than background at this point.
- Have a firm handshake, shake the hand of every board member, look them in the eye, and greet them by name.
- If the interview is in public, touch as many people as possible on your way in. Make sure you don't overlook greeting school children, the elderly, or people with mobility challenges who may be present and not able to get to you.
- Make eye contact with interviewers and the audience. Don't focus on the table or the ceiling when you talk.
- Have a pleasant smile, be confident and calm—no matter how nervous you are! Get all of your butterflies flying in the same direction.
- Maintain a strong, but not overbearing voice.

- Develop a "killer" opening statement. They will generally always start with a softball "tell us about yourself" question. This is the time to tell your 5-7 minute leadership story. It is not the time to rehash your chronological resume. Connect with them as a person—share with them who you are, what has made you what you are, what in your life has brought you to this district at this point in time. Selectively present pertinent facts organized in a confident, focused manner. Tell your story! Make a connection! (See my monograph *In the Arena* for more information on developing your leadership story.)

The Rest of the Interview

Although they may be worded differently, typical question areas are likely to include:
- Success in the area of student achievement
- Leadership/management experience
- Board relations and experience
- Vision and strategy
- Community engagement
- Political experience
- Financial management
- Establishing accountability and assessing performance
- Conflict management skills
- Experience with diverse populations
- Experience with unions
- Why you want this job and what you can bring to it

Sample interview questions are included in Appendix E. If you can answer them and be current on local, state and national issues, you should be prepared for just about any question they might ask.

No matter how they word the question, in each area, the board will want to hear:
- that first and foremost you are all about kids and doing what's right for them
- that your prior experience has prepared you to deal with the issues their district is facing
- you've had some success and experience dealing with these issues or parallel issues in a related field

- what you believe about their current challenges and opportunities
- how you will work with them and the staff to address their needs
- that through your work, you'll enhance their political standing and image in the community

This part (the rest of the interview) may last an hour. The challenge is to hold people's attention for the entire hour and not lose your energy and momentum. Here are some tips for doing that:
- Modulate your voice
- Be appropriately reflective before responding to selected questions—don't appear over-prepared
- Provide complete, adequate responses without rambling—limit your answers to no more than 3-5 minutes per response; state the bottom line, then expand on it a bit
- Use appropriate, self-effacing humor; relax and smile— candidates tend to take themselves far too seriously
- Change your position occasionally
- Talk conversationally, not as if you were giving a college lecture
- Direct your answer to the entire board—not just the member posing the question
- Relate answers back to student achievement and the interests of children, to as great an extent as possible
- Reference the strengths, challenges, and opportunities of their system in your responses
- Sell yourself—don't be shy about your accomplishments, but don't overstate the facts
- Appropriately demonstrate your interest in the job, but leave them feeling like they need you more than you need them
- Believe in your own myths! We are all the hero of our own story.
- Be positive about the future of their system, be bold, be humble, be all about kids!

The Final Ten Minutes

Make them remember you. After they've interviewed six people, you want to leave them with a "takeaway" impression they won't easily forget.
- They'll give you an opportunity to ask a question or two. Ask them the "softball" questions you have prepared.
- Ask for the opportunity to make a closing statement if none is offered. Take the opportunity if none is granted. This may be the

time to revisit a particular question with something you wish you had said the first time.
- Deliver your "killer" closing statement. It should connect to your opening statement and key points in the interview, and connect you to their district and their needs.
- Acknowledge the importance and difficulty of their decision-making process.
- Thank them and the community members present for the opportunity to speak with them. Wish them well in this most critical of all decision-making processes they will engage in on behalf of their children.

One of the best closing statements I've heard came from the successful candidate for a large urban district with a notoriously dysfunctional board that publicly exhibited infighting and other inappropriate behavior. He had a great second interview and was neck-and-neck with another candidate. He chose to conclude his interview with a challenge to the board that went something like this:

"I want to wrap up my time with you by saying what a pleasure it has been to go through this process. I've enjoyed meeting each and every one of you, the members of your staff, and the community. I've particularly enjoyed the opportunity to meet and learn more about your incredible students. I have to tell you that I would love to be your next superintendent, and I believe that working together we could accomplish great things for the children of this community. But I have to tell you that it hasn't gone unnoticed that over the past couple of years, this board has gotten a lot of headlines in the local media—for the wrong reasons. Your inability to work well together and with your outgoing superintendent has become a distraction to the work going on in the district.

While I want to be your next superintendent, I don't want to be part of a dysfunctional governance team that continues that legacy. So, I would ask that should you consider me worthy of this appointment, please don't come to me with that offer unless you're going to renew your commitment to work together in a spirit of cooperation and support. Let me be clear. I'm not just talking about a civil tolerance of each other, but actually doing the work necessary to place this board's best foot forward on behalf of the children who are counting on us. Within six months of my

64

appointment, I want to be able to tape every single board meeting and send those tapes to our ninth grade civics teachers so that they can show their students a model of how a governing body in a democracy should work.

If you're willing to make that commitment, and you want me to be a member of your team, that will be my commitment as well. Please accept my best wishes as you conclude this critical decision-making process, and thank you again for the opportunity to be considered."

The audience immediately burst into a raucous standing ovation, and the job was his.

Second Interview with the Board and School Community

If there were ever a time to bring your "A" game, this is it. If this is a public process, second interviews are generally day-long marathon affairs. They may start at 7:30 am and end at 10:00 pm, with several public forums, individual meetings, and interviews scheduled in between.

Forums with Constituent Groups

During the day, you may have separate forums scheduled with teachers, administrative staff, community groups, business leaders, parent groups, and student groups. The forums may be up to an hour each.

- Bring fresh energy to each and every group, even though it may be the tenth group you've met with during the day.
- They want to know four simple things:
    - Who you are—your 5-10 minute leadership story
    - Your passion for and commitment to serving kids
    - How you will include them, work with them, and treat them
    - Why you want to serve their community as superintendent of schools at this point in time
- Have a few "softball" questions prepared to ask them as well. These should be questions that put them in touch with their feelings about kids and their hopes for the district. Don't ask technical questions unless you're dealing specifically with the technician who should have the answers.

- You will need to find a way to connect with each group on a personal level. Be yourself in the context of their needs.
- Be mentally prepared for anything.
- Smile, Smile, Smile!

You may also be given tours of the district schools. Be sure to take time to talk to the support staff, as well as students and teachers. If a building is very clean, ask to meet the custodian. Don't miss the opportunity to meet cafeteria workers and bus drivers and let them know their work is important to you.

Assume that <u>everything</u> you say and do will make it back to the board. Remain focused and on point. Board members may be present at several or all of your meetings during the day. If not, they will have someone appointed to report back to them on your performance.

Board Interview

The day will usually end with an interview with the board that is less structured than the first, generally lasting about an hour. They will want to ask you any of their unanswered questions and try to decide if you are someone they can work with. They will be coming to a conclusion about whether you are someone who will enhance their standing in the community and someone they would like to spend a considerable amount of time with over the weeks, months, and years ahead.

This is the time to be prepared with more pointed questions you may have for the board. If you have lingering concerns about how they might work with you, or concerns about how they will work toward resolution of challenging issues before them, now is the time to ask. Once again, having a closing statement that incites their passion for doing the right things for kids is key.

District Visitation – the Final Snapshot

Some boards may decide that they need to "see for themselves" and conduct a site visit to your current district or place of employment. This is done more often in smaller and mid-size districts than in large districts, but is still a common practice.

The down side to a site visit is the disruption it can cause in your current place of employment. If you are a sitting superintendent and you are not the sole, final candidate, it may be risky to put your school and community through the ordeal. You should find out early on whether this will be part of the process and make the search consultant aware of any non-negotiables you may have in this area. For example, if, as a sitting superintendent, you are not willing to host a board visitation unless you are the only finalist, your search firm rep needs to know this before the board selects finalists.

The up side of the visit is that you are generally in charge of organizing the day and usually have the final say over the specific people with whom the board members will meet. So your task is to arrange a great experience for the board representatives.

They will want to talk to several people about their impressions of your leadership:
- Your supervisor and/or board members
- Your direct reports
- Principals, teachers
- Union representatives
- Business community
- Students, parents

However the day is scheduled, be sure it ends on a high note with your most powerful and strongest advocates meeting with them at the conclusion of their visit, just before you have your final discussion with them.

If You Are an Internal Candidate

If you are an internal candidate for a superintendency, you still need to prepare for the application and interview process as described above. Think like an outsider from the very beginning. Use the strengths of your inside knowledge of the district, but don't assume anything.

At the beginning of the search process, the search consultant will usually have a discussion with the board about internal candidates. If the board feels there are strong, viable candidates within the organization, they have a couple options.

If there is a "natural successor" that will be accepted by all constituencies, the board may just post internally, interview and appoint the person.

If they feel one or more constituencies may not be happy with the person's appointment, the board may decide to have a full process and make insiders compete with outside candidates. This can actually serve to strengthen an internal candidate's "legitimacy" if they ultimately get the job.

In some situations, boards may appoint a strong internal candidate as the interim superintendent while the search is conducted. Unless the board is simply doing a trial run with the internal candidate for the real job, search firms may discourage the board from appointing a prospective candidate to the interim role. It makes it far more difficult to recruit a quality field of candidates if the board had made this "tip of their hand" in support of an internal person. If, as the internal candidate, you find yourself in the position of interim, take the job seriously and demonstrate your capacity to lead the system.

Internal candidates should be careful throughout the process and not let their friends and supporters inadvertently kill their candidacy by lobbying the board too heavily.

SUPERINTENDENT CONTRACT NEGOTIATION

Congratulations! You've been offered the job! This chapter outlines the key factors new superintendents should consider when negotiating their initial employment contract with a district. This is not intended to provide a comprehensive guide to the superintendent's contract, but rather serve as a primer to create awareness of key topics and ensure your appropriate focus during the negotiation process.

The Context for Negotiations

It is important to understand the context for contract negotiation. Each district will be different, and each situation different. Before engaging in the process, consider:

- The contract of your predecessor—this is a public document, and it is fair game to ask for a copy
- Your professional career and compensation needs—what do you need for base pay? What retirement fund needs do you have? How important is job security to you at this stage of your career?
- Compensation parameters communicated to you during the candidate recruitment and application phase of the process
- Salaries and total compensation of superintendents in comparable peer districts
- The financial condition of the district and the state
- The relative cost of living in the district as compared to your current location (several online tools are available for this)
- Compensation ranges of the board members and other local public officials
- When contract negotiation is occurring in the selection process—obviously, you have the most bargaining power if you have already been publicly named as the board's unanimous choice

The Negotiation Process

Depending upon the size and complexity of the district, the board may have an attorney involved in the process—you should, too. Identify an attorney who has experience with superintendent contracts rather than simply using your family attorney.

Either you and the board president or your representative attorneys will agree on the basic terms and then will discuss the basic contract parameters. If the board chair indicates that, "We'll let the attorneys negotiate the contract," then, if at all possible, have your attorney present the initial draft contract. This way you can better control the framework, context, and tone of the contract language.

It is important to keep the process moving and make sure your attorney is responsive. You don't want the contact negotiations to drag on long enough to become a public issue—you'll run the risk of burning your pot of political capital before you even start the job.

Treat your first contract as if it were your last contract. In other words, don't plan on being able to negotiate better terms in future contracts, particularly in challenging financial times or if you're going into a troubled situation and know you'll need to make controversial decisions.

And know that the terms of your contract will inevitably become public information—include only what you can live with (politically and on the front page of the newspaper) in this community.

Customary Contractual Clauses

Following are typical clauses found in superintendent contracts, with important considerations noted for each. Most state superintendent associations provide model contract language which should be available on their web site or by request.

Introductory Clause
This clause simply states that this is an agreement between the board and the superintendent. Make sure you are appointed as superintendent and not the administrator, and don't let the board have the right to reassign you to another position.

Duties
There may be a general statement of your duties as superintendent, probably as dictated by state law or perhaps by board policy. This section may also include a statement about maintaining certification requirements. Make sure you understand the respective laws, policies, and requirements referenced.

Management Rights
This is an important section to negotiate into your contract. Try to obtain the authority to organize and reorganize district staff and to hire and fire staff (especially your executive team). Ensure that <u>all</u> district staff report to you and none report directly to the board.

Ensure that the superintendent has the right to attend all board meetings and board committee meetings except those executive sessions where the board is considering your performance or your contract.

You may be able to negotiate language that restricts board interference into operational matters and includes consequences if the clause is violated, although this is rare.

Term of Contract and Contract Renewal
The term of a superintendent's contract will normally be between three and five years. You will be leaving a good job to come to this district, moving your family, and probably selling a home. They should not expect you to accept a lesser commitment from them. You may try to seek an "evergreen" clause that states the contract will automatically be extended annually by one additional year if the board does not take any action to the contrary by a specific date each year.

> *"Money can't buy happiness, but it can buy you the kind of misery you prefer."*
> *(Author Unknown)*

Termination
The reason for your termination may be for "just cause" or for no cause. Think about where you are in your career, anticipate that your relationship with this board will not last forever, and figure out how you want it to play out when it is time for you to leave—a clean separation, or messy and public?

Whether for just cause or no cause, try to include a minimum buyout amount if the board wants you to leave prior to the end of your contract. You will want enough to provide a financial cushion to allow you to find another position and move to a new community. If the payout is too large, the board may look foolish to the public, you will look greedy, and it may hurt you in your future job searches.

Performance Evaluation
The specific process for your evaluation will probably not be laid out in the contract, but be sure it includes a commitment to agree upon a process no later than the conclusion of your first ninety days on the job. Try to obtain a contractual commitment to quarterly formative assessments and an annual summative evaluation.

Do not agree to being evaluated on district performance metrics during your first year; that should begin in Year Two. Do not agree to be evaluated using any numerical rating scale. I've seen too many superintendents have a great first year, receiving an overall rating of 4.9 on a 5 point scale. By Year Two, they may have a couple new board members who rate a little differently, and they will have had to make some tough decisions, so the rating may come out to a 4.2, inviting the local paper to report that "Superintendent Performance Slips!" This is not productive, and doesn't invite substantive conversation about the superintendent's performance. (See our monograph *Peak Performing Governance Teams* for more information on this topic.)

Compensation
Your total compensation includes a combination of base salary and additional financial compensation factors. There are more than a dozen ways to receive additional financial compensation over and above base salary, which is typically the figure quoted in the media. Be sure to find out how the additional compensation factors may be taxed and will factor into this state's retirement system calculations.

Additional financial enhancements may include:
- Performance bonus pay—while this is becoming increasingly common and it sets the stage for district-wide accountability, think through the politics of this. Be sure funds are earmarked in the budget if you go this route; funds may be held in a district reserve for future payment if necessary. Receiving a bonus in tough financial times can make you look greedy, and may do more harm than good.
- Deferred compensation—contributions to a supplemental retirement annuity
- Longevity
- Professional leave days, allowing you to do consulting on these days of paid leave
- Additional vacation days, reimbursable if not used

72

- Personal leave days, reimbursable if not used
- Research and study sabbatical, cumulative and reimbursable if not taken
- Life insurance—purchase of universal or whole life policy with annual deposit of cash value in your name
- Purchase of years in state retirement system—i.e., district buys one additional year for each year of service to the district
- Reimbursement for superintendent's contribution to social security
- Lifetime family health benefits—to begin accruing after x years of service
- Paid consulting days in the district prior to your official start date if the board wants you to spend some transition time there

Fringe Benefits
Superintendents are usually awarded whatever other administrators in the district get as a basis. These typically include:
- Health, dental, vision, life, disability insurance
- Sick days
- Vacation days (payout for unused days and, perhaps, additional days are common—given the fact that your work schedule is often 24x7)
- Retirement plan

If an annual medical exam at board expense is included, the detailed results should not go to the board—simply a statement indicating that you either are or are not fit to do the work.

"It's easy to make a buck. It's a lot tougher to make a difference."
(Tom Brokaw)

Additional Services Provided
The district will usually provide the superintendent with appropriate computing and communication technology.

The superintendent is usually provided with transportation. I advise receiving a flat allowance for a vehicle rather than driving a district-owned car; there is no question about who can drive it, where it is driven, or accurate reporting of personal and business mileage. If a flat allowance is not in the cards, the district normally covers the cost of maintenance, fuel, and insurance in addition to the lease or purchase cost; be sure personal use of the vehicle is allowed.

In some situations, it may be the norm for the superintendent to have a car and driver provided; in other contexts, that may be way "over the top." In some smaller districts, simple reimbursement for out-of-district travel expenses is the only thing that makes sense.

Personal security protection may also be provided by the district, depending on the context.

Relocation or Transition Expenses
Moving expenses for the new superintendent are typically covered in some fashion, in a contract addendum. This can be a flat amount, the lesser of three bids, or other formula.

The district may posture that moving expenses will be covered only if the superintendent moves into the district. Depending upon the economic climate, boards may agree to cover the cost of temporary housing, or some other housing transition "hold harmless" arrangement.

The costs of all post-selection/pre-start date visits to the district which are requested or encouraged by the board are also often compensated by the district.

Professional Liability
The district should provide professional liability insurance for the superintendent. Include appropriate hold harmless and indemnification language. Ensure that the district pays any legal fees for the superintendent if involved in a suit, dispute or negotiation stemming from this job during and following the term of the contract.

Professional Growth
If you plan to do any outside consulting, be sure to spell out this understanding. Include district payment of appropriate professional dues or memberships in local, state or national organizations and travel to annual conferences or meetings as necessary.

Remember, seek legal counsel, use common sense, negotiate in the context of your needs, but also in the context of the district's fiscal and political climate.

TRANSITION PLANNING

When transitioning out of your current position and into a new, you need to carefully plan your departure. No matter how you feel about your old organization, a professional departure will serve you well for the rest of your career. Handled poorly, a bad ending can come back to haunt you, time and time again. The old adage about not burning bridges is a good one.

Communicate

When you begin to apply for other positions, you'll need to communicate with some key people. There are few secrets in this field, and there are some people you do not want to be surprised by learning of your candidacy from another source:

- *Your current supervisor or employer.* Have a frank discussion with your supervisor about your plans. Solicit his/her support and commitment to serve as a reference. If your supervisor can't support your candidacy, at least try to gain a commitment that he/she won't block it. Ideally, you would have had conversations with your supervisor before this point about your career aspirations, so this shouldn't be a shock.
- *Professional references.* Let them know the position you are applying for, and alert them that they may be receiving a call. You may also want to remind them of your qualities or experiences they might be able to attest to in the context of the desired position. When the search consultant calls references, a prepared reference always does a better job on your behalf. It's your job to prepare them.
- *Any others whom you don't want to be surprised.* Let these folks know at the appropriate point in the process, before information is to be made public. These may include key direct reports and others with whom you've worked closely and would be most directly affected by your departure.

Leave a Better Situation

If at all possible, don't leave any messes for your successor to clean up. Make sure you are leaving your position and your office in order and in better condition than when you arrived and in a condition that enhances the possibility of success for whomever might follow you.

It is a common courtesy to prepare an exit report for your successor and your supervisor. This report would include:
- An outline of the key responsibilities of the position
- An outline of key accomplishments during your tenure
- A briefing on the key initiatives under way and plans for their implementation
- Any potential pitfalls or challenges on the horizon
- Contact information where you can be reached if needed

Departing with Class

There are a few relationship-building actions you need to take at this time:

> *"The only thing you take with you when you're gone is what you leave behind."*
> *(John Allston)*

- Make an appropriate statement for your local media, praising your current organization and its staff.
- Mend your fences. If you've developed some "enemies," now is the time to extend a peace offering. Thank them for being a "worthy adversary" and for challenging you to be a better leader.
- Burn no bridges. You may be tempted to take some parting shots as you walk out the door. You never know when you'll cross someone's path again and need their support.
- Honor and thank those who have helped in your success. You didn't accomplish anything alone. Let those who supported you know they are appreciated.
- Make a congratulatory call to your successor. Offer your support to them, but….
- Avoid meddling in your successor's business. You may get calls from prior staff or board members who are frustrated with the new directions and new ways of doing business. Your involvement in these matters doesn't help anyone through the transition.

Promote Yourself

Acknowledge the fact that you are going to be going through a major career and personal transition. The best way to handle this is to establish a clear breakpoint for when you let go of the old and embrace the new. Then take some time to celebrate.

You also need to acknowledge that you are going into a new situation. In addition to taking on a new role, you may be entering a new organization or a new state. The biggest mistake people make is to think that the skills that got you here will be all you need to be successful in the future. Take some time to think about what you need to learn or do differently:

- Assess your vulnerabilities. What new skills will you need to succeed? What current areas of strength or responsibility will you need to let go? For example, if you are a strong CFO, as superintendent you'll need to be able to delegate that area and focus on the entire organization.
- Relearn how to learn. Perhaps you've been in professional "auto-pilot" for the past few years and think you know everything under the sun. Maybe you don't go to conferences because "there is nothing anyone can teach me that I don't already know." Model professional growth and learning. You'll soon discover as superintendent that you don't know it all. Remember that in your new role you are the first learner and the first teacher in the organization.
- Restructure your professional network. The superintendency can be a lonely job. You'll no longer be able to confide with peers within the organization. Therefore, you'll need to connect with other superintendents and CEOs in your region and in similar districts. Identify the best and seek their counsel.

Prepare for the Media Blitz

As soon as you are announced as the new superintendent, expect to be pressed by the media immediately. Be ready.

Being well prepared for the interview process will be helpful with this. Be sure you understand the history and issues of your new district. Be able to tell your story in the context of this new community. Make sure that as you communicate, you are:

- All about kids
- Authentic
- Honest
- All about kids
- Humble

- Bold
- Optimistic
- All about kids

Honoring the Past

Don't make the mistake of criticizing your predecessor or prior failures of the organization. Even if accurate, it is generally perceived as "classless." In addition, many people who contributed to those failed initiatives are still in the organization. Trash-talking their prior efforts won't win their support as you go forward.

Remember that your predecessor was dealing with a different time, a different set of circumstances, different perspectives, and different players. Assume that everyone gave their best effort as they best knew how. The situation has now changed, and you'll deal with it in new ways.

Don't entertain the "bearers of horror and gore." Some people will delight in sharing with you all the horrible things that went on in the past administration. Just be aware that they will do the same thing to you after you are gone.

OFF TO A GREAT START: PLAN OF ENTRY

Now let's turn our focus to having a great start as superintendent. It is almost always apparent during the new superintendent's first 90-100 days on the job whether their tenure will be a brief exercise of frustration or if it will be long, fruitful and productive for kids and the community. **Having a successful first 90 days is critical to having a successful first year. Having a successful first year is critical to having a successful tenure.**

Listed below are activities designed to help a new superintendent gather information quickly about the district and the community, establish a positive community presence early on, and create a network of contacts and resources to tap as he or she enters the new role. All activities may or may not be appropriate in a given community, but should at least be considered.

The ideas are suggested for the new superintendent's "private" list of entry actions. You should also develop a "public" plan of entry to share with the board, staff and community. This would be a public relations document outlining entry objectives and providing an overview of activities to be undertaken, rather than a detailed to-do list. This can be called a "Plan of Entry," a "Listening and Learning Plan," an "Orientation Plan," or similar name. You may also choose to adopt a "theme" for this entry process that will start to identify your primary focus as superintendent. Examples are *"Excellence and Equity"* or *"Every Child Achieves."*

Prior To Start Date

From the date of selection to the actual start date in the district, several activities should be conducted.
- Conclude contract negotiations (see chapter on superintendent's contract)
- Complete and review your district research
- Review all board policies and administrative policies and procedures
- Review any recent district, school, program, or functional area audits or studies
- Review most recent financial audits and management letters

- Draft personal and public plan of entry; ask trusted advisors for feedback
- Schedule and conduct one-on-one interviews with each board member
- Schedule and conduct one-on-one interviews with each of your direct reports
- Schedule your first retreat with the board to occur within 30 days of your first day on the job—either before or after. Be prepared to state your expectations of the board and to learn of their initial and long-term expectations for your performance. (See draft agenda for a first board retreat in our monograph *Peak Performing Governance Teams.*)
- Schedule your first retreat with your leadership team (your direct reports) within your first 10 days on the job.

First Day On the Job

A superintendent makes both technical and symbolic decisions. Few things are more importantly symbolic than how a new superintendent spends the first day on the job. This day will be highly visible, both inside the organization and within the community. You need to decide what the initial focus of your superintendency will be, and arrange visible activities supporting that focus—everyone will be watching, so, in districts where appropriate, invite the media to come along. Will you be riding buses at 6:30 am? Will you spend time in classrooms? Will you meet with principals? Meet with business leaders? Or will you be arranging furniture in your office? It all sends a message. Keep in mind that if you begin at the traditional start date of July 1, you will have that symbolic first day on the job plus the first day that kids are present. Both should be planned thoughtfully.

> *"The President of the United States gets 100 days to prove himself; you get 90. The actions you take during your first three months in a new job will largely determine whether you succeed or fail."*
> *(Michael Watkins)*

The First 90 Days on the Job

Getting acquainted with a new organization can feel like drinking from a fire hose. Your goals during this first critical time period are:

- Effective, efficient, strategic learning about all facets of the district
- Generating as much political capital as possible
- Creating political cover for making necessary changes (the information you uncover with your fresh look at the organization can serve as the rationale for moving in new directions)

To help manage and organize everything that needs to be done, it is most useful to establish objectives and outline activities in five key areas:
- Governance team
- Organizational capacity and alignment
- Student achievement
- Community and public engagement
- Operations and finance

Governance Team

Your Purpose: Establish working relationships with individual board members and the board as a whole.

Potential Activities:
- Review board election calendar
- Conduct one-on-one interviews with each board member (see a sample interview format and protocols in Appendix F)
- Meet with the board president and board committee chairs to determine how they work together and with the superintendent
- Hold the first quarterly retreat within 30 days of your start date—either before or after
- Determine the schedule for quarterly or periodic board retreats

Organizational Capacity and Alignment

Your Purpose: Establish a strong and appropriately focused district executive or leadership team.

Potential Activities:
- Thoroughly review district's strategic plan, planning process, accountability or performance management system, and project management structure
- Review resumes of people in top district staff positions

- Request briefing papers from all direct reports providing an overview of their current area of responsibility, major initiatives under way with projected time lines, significant or potential problems in each area of responsibility, and major decisions that need to be made in one month, three months and six months
- Conduct one-on-one interviews with all direct reports (see sample interview format and protocols in Appendix G)
- Review the central office organizational structure
- Review current or anticipated vacancies in administrative staffing and develop plans for filling those positions
- Determine how communication and decision-making will occur (vs. how it always has been done)
- Establish leadership team standards of practice and communication protocols

Student Achievement

Your Purpose: Understand current strategies, strengths and opportunities for improvement in the district's teaching and learning program.

Potential Activities:
- Meet with district's instructional leadership team to discuss achievement data, instructional program alignment, current performance metrics, and priority action areas for the district
- Assess the current professional development program, paying particular attention to the current capacity and the training needs of principals, teachers, and senior district staff
- Review alignment of the central office in support of student achievement
- Review district accountability plan for instructional areas first and all other functional areas second

Community and Public Relations

Your Purpose: Meet community, political and parent organization leaders to learn community perspectives, generate good will, build support, and establish critical communication channels.

Potential Activities:

- Consider hosting "town hall meetings" with as many key constituency groups (parents, teachers, business leaders, and student leaders) as necessary for the community to feel that they have been heard. At these focus group-type sessions, you would share your leadership story and ask the group to help identify the district's Strengths and Challenges. Be prepared to effectively process and capture their input. Invite individual board members to accompany you to each of these sessions.
- Visit various local community groups, perhaps accompanied by individual school board members
- One-on-one meetings with all top-level locally elected officials and community leaders (see sample format and protocols for these initial interviews in Appendix H)
- One-on-one meetings with all area legislators (state and national)
- One-on-one meetings with members of the legislature's education committee, the chief state school officer and the Governor's point-person on education (if you are in a high-profile district in your state)
- Meet the county/regional superintendent of schools and the county/regional board of education
- If you are in a new state, ask the district's legal counsel to brief you on the state education code, with particular attention paid to statutes currently impacting or likely to impact the district during your first year on the job
- Meet with the heads of the teacher, administrator, non-classified, and other unions; establish a regular means of communication and mutual expectations for the conduct of business with union leaders
- Meet one-on-one with leaders of the major local media outlets and with editorial boards of newspapers, including the ethnic and business press where applicable
- Invite TV, radio and newspaper reporters to appropriate community sessions in the first 90 days
- Conduct a review of the district's public information office and programs if applicable; review the history, services and experience of the community liaison office
- Understand the district's crisis communications plan

Operations and Finance

Your Purpose: Understand the current strategies, strengths and opportunities for improvement in the district's operations and finance areas

Potential Activities:
- Review district financial audits for the last three years, financial projections, resource allocation and budgeting processes; assess how district's budget and budgeting process are aligned to support student achievement
- Review all pending legal proceedings or other prospective judgments
- Review all employee group contracts including expiration dates and plans for negotiation of renewals
- Understand district's information technology systems and plans for the future
- Understand district accountability plan for operational areas
- Review and understand district safety and emergency plans

80 – 90 Days on the Job

Near the end of the first 90 days, you will have learned a great deal about the district, formed impressions of the current status, and developed initial ideas regarding new directions for the future.

A second board retreat should be held toward the conclusion of the first 90 days. At this retreat, you will present an entry plan report outlining your findings and proposed plans/agenda for the remainder of the first year. These proposed plans should also be effectively communicated with the school community to obtain their understanding, buy-in and support. You need to be bold and confident about achieving a better future! But remember, this is no time to damn the past or its owners—build upon it.

Some General Advice

During this initial 90 days, you should be looking for some early wins ("low hanging fruit.") These will be some easier or symbolic actions you can take that will demonstrate your ability to execute.

One of these initial actions may be fixing obvious safety or security problems. Another may be replacement of ineffective members of your leadership team. People in the organization know who these folks are— they're just watching you to see if you can spot them, too. Don't keep existing leadership team members too long if it is clear they won't work out. Competence, trustworthiness, and commitment to your agenda should be your key criteria in this assessment.

You will be meeting with many people during this time period. Be sure that in each group or one-on-one meeting you are focused. They should get the message that:

- Your #1 priority is student achievement
- You care about them as partners
- You know your business
- You are a good listener
- Your #1 priority is student achievement

Finally, recognize that this is a huge transition for you professionally and personally. Your first 90 days will, of necessity, be a time of imbalance in your life. Be sure to schedule time to take care of yourself physically, spiritually, socially, and emotionally. Make sure that you don't neglect the most important people in your life. Schedule family commitments on your calendar and keep those commitments. I recommend that after the first three months, you should calendar—and honor—one three-day weekend per month with significant others, as well as plans for holidays and summer vacation.

FORMING A KITCHEN CABINET

Wise leaders seek the independent and private counsel of other leaders, influencers, or experts. They create an unofficial "Kitchen Cabinet" in order to:

- Gain perspective on issues
- Expand their knowledge and political awareness
- Help evaluate ideas, develop strategies and probe problems
- Seek unique viewpoints on old problems
- Seek new ideas
- Develop relationships that may be helpful in navigating political challenges

During your plan of entry, you should meet the key players in your community. You should be using this opportunity to begin to identify the members of your Kitchen Cabinet. You'll know who these people are because in every interview you'll be asking for the names of people you should be talking to and listening to. (See Appendix H.)

Successful superintendents understand the need to make these types of connections. Use of a Kitchen Cabinet is covered in more depth in my monograph *Peak Performing Governance Teams*.

I first fully appreciated the potential of creating and nurturing a kitchen cabinet after hearing the story of one superintendent. He took the job on a 5-2 vote, and, at the very next meeting, one of the dissenting votes was elected board chair. It just so happened that this board member was also a vice president of the community's largest bank, and was a direct report to the founder and president of the bank, one of the most influential people in the community. In the superintendent's first interview with the board chair, he asked the question, "Who in your opinion, are the most important people in the community I should be scheduling meetings with during my orientation into the district?" The board chair immediately identified his boss. The superintendent asked if he'd be willing to arrange a meeting for him, and he was more than pleased to do so. The meeting was scheduled to last for 15 minutes, and the board chair escorted the superintendent to his boss's door. To his chagrin, his boss thanked him for bringing the superintendent to the office, and then dismissed him. The meeting lasted for almost two hours. At its conclusion, the bank president said, "You know, I really like you and want you to be successful here. I want you to

87

know that if your new board chair creates any problems for you, let me know and I'll take care of it for you."

The lesson here is that the movers and shakers in the community want a relationship with the person who is leading their school system, and they can be very helpful in managing the sometimes delicate issues of board and community politics.

FIRST YEAR MILESTONES

As you think about your first year, there are several critical milestones you should not miss.

Prior to Your First Day
- Complete your district research
- Develop your Plan of Entry
- Plan your activities for your first day on the job
- Conduct your one-on-one interviews with board members and direct reports, if at all possible

Within Your First Month on the Job
- Hold your first retreat with the board, if not conducted prior to your start date. Gain agreement on your communication protocols and standards of practice. Share key elements of your Plan of Entry. (See our monograph *Peak Performing Governance Teams* for more information on this retreat agenda.)
- Conduct your first retreat with your leadership team. Gain agreement on your communication protocols and standards of practice.
- Begin to execute your Plan of Entry.

At the End of Your First 90 Days
- Conclude your Plan of Entry activities. Summarize your findings and recommendations for moving forward; share with the board in retreat. Obviously, the media and public will also need a briefing on your findings and recommendations.
- By this time you should have reached agreement with the board on the criteria and process by which you will be evaluated during your first year.

Six - Nine Months on the Job
- Review and update the district's strategic plan, including metrics of success for your second year on the job.
- Hold your third quarterly retreat with the board; obtain formative feedback on your performance, review governance team performance pertaining to communication protocols and standards of practice.

At the End of Your First Year
- Hold your fourth quarterly retreat with the board, receiving a summative evaluation of your first year performance.

At this point you will have achieved the vision laid out in the very beginning of this monograph:

> *You've gotten the job of your dreams and are approaching the end of the first year in your new role. Your board has just completed your first annual evaluation. They have overwhelmed you with praise and heartfelt gratitude for your good work on behalf of children. They voted unanimously to extend your contract for three years and to award you not only a cost of living increase in salary, but a performance bonus as well. This was quite an impressive first year, and should lay the foundation for many more productive years to come.*

CONCLUDING THOUGHTS

In summary, once you've determined that the superintendency is right for you and have then determined if a particular district may be a good fit, you'll make a decision to either sit tight or apply.

If you decide to apply, you have submitted yourself to a competition with anywhere from a dozen to 150 other players, and there will only be one winner. To use a sports analogy—*if you're not ready to compete to win, don't play.* If you do decide to play, approach the process as a campaign. Understand how the rules of this particular game will be applied. Know when and how this particular process will end. Understand more than any other candidate about the specific prize you are pursuing.

Know the officials guiding the process and those making the decisions. Know who your competitors are, to as great an extent as possible. I emphasize this last point because in the final stages of the interview process, you may need to juxtapose your skills and talents against theirs in the context of this district's needs. Your primary emphasis, however, should be on yourself and the good you can do for the district's children, rather than on the competition.

In addition to doing all of the homework I've recommended, get yourself in the best physical condition of your life—it will influence your confidence, improve your presence, and provide the additional energy you'll need to get through a grueling process—and master the challenging first year on the job.

In the end, no matter how the process concludes, make sure that you can look yourself in the mirror and say that you gave it your best effort.

If you have not "won the game," review what you've learned from the experience. Process those learnings with a trusted advisor, and begin to contemplate the next possibility. Understand that there may be a rational reason the board felt the other candidate was a better fit—or accept the fact that governing bodies are made up of human beings who sometimes make irrational decisions. Adopt the attitude that things happen for a reason, and that reason will be revealed to you in the months and years ahead.

If you've won the job, get off to a great start, as it will lay a solid foundation for a long and successful tenure.

APPENDIX

DETERMINING DISTRICT FIT

Use this form to help think through the types of districts that would be a good fit for you.

Priority:
5 = absolute must
4 = a big plus factor
3 = would be nice
2 = not very important
1 = not at all important

Current District Status:
5 = excellent
4 = good
3 = average
2 = weak
1 = poor

Factors to Consider	Priority	Current District Status	Notes:
Geographic location			
Setting for children/spouse			
Similar commitment to student achievement for all children			
Similar beliefs regarding how to achieve success			
A good leadership team, or ability to select own executive staff			
Readiness for change			
Openness to someone with my experience, style and characteristics			
Quality of instructional program			
Quality of operational systems			
Financial condition			

Factors to Consider	Priority	Current Status	Notes:
Condition of facilities			
Political environment			
Community values			
Quality of board members			
Board/mayoral support			
Board working relationships			
Compensation package			
Other			
Other			

DISTRICT RESEARCH STARTER QUESTIONS

Candidates should research the answers to these questions prior to applying for a position.

Demographic and Community Information:
- Number of students
- Racial and ethnic breakdown of students, staff and community
- Percentage of economically disadvantaged students
- Number of teachers, administrators, and non-certified staff
- 5 major employers in community

Student Achievement:
- Student achievement scores, achievement gaps and trends
- Percentage of students who go on to college, by race, gender, economic status
- Percentage of students in special education, by race, gender, economic status
- Dropout/retention rates, by race, gender, economic status

Governance:
- Governance structure – elected or appointed board
- Names of board members, tenure of each member and what they do for a living
- Existence and content of board standards of practice and board/superintendent relationship policies
- Policies on board orientation and professional growth

Political Environment:
- Labor relations climate and issues
- Which employee groups are unionized and which unions represent them
- Labor contract with teachers union (can be found online in many states)
- Community political climate and issues
- Local media outlets – search for district news in prior year
- Major philanthropic organizations in the community

Organization and Management:
- District vision, mission, guiding beliefs, strategic plan
- District indicators and measures of success
- District accountability/performance management plan
- Organizational chart

Operations:
- Annual budget and most recent annual financial audit report
- Fund balance and changes to fund balance over past 5 years
- Per pupil expenditure
- Pie charts on district expenditures and revenues
- Bonded indebtedness
- Number and age of facilities

Career Issues:
- Last three superintendents, their length of tenure, and why each left
- Internal candidates for the position
- Retirement plan of the district or state in which the district is located, and how your current retirement plan would be impacted if you were to move to this district
- Approximate salary the position will pay
- Compare cost of living with your current city (several websites can calculate this)

SAMPLE APPLICATION COVER LETTER

Date

Address Block

Dear X:

Please accept my application to be the next Superintendent of the Middle City Public Schools.

This position interests me for several reasons. My family has strong roots in the Middle City area, and I still consider the community our "home base." My grandparents both attended Jefferson Elementary School and shared many fond memories of the East End community. While the District certainly has challenges to face, it is exciting that the Middle City Schools has such strong support from its community and business partners. I believe there is great potential for this district to achieve unprecedented levels of success. It would be both challenging and rewarding to "come home" and work with the school community in making this success happen.

Presently, I am Deputy Superintendent of the Rust Belt City School District. The district has 15,600 students, 65% of whom live in poverty. It is also a highly diverse district, with 70% African American, 15% Hispanic and 15% white students. My background in Rust Belt City has provided me with the expertise and preparation necessary to be Superintendent of the Middle City Public Schools.

Schools under my leadership have made several lasting improvements including improved student achievement, updated facilities, aligned curriculum, additional programs for English Language Learners, and great technological advancements. This was all achieved by establishing a clear vision for the schools, setting high expectations, and inspiring everyone to work together toward these goals. I am confident that I can provide the same kind of leadership and expertise for the Middle City School District so that, together, we can build upon the quality programs already in place.

In my present role, I had the responsibility of being the lead communicator for our district's $25 million bond issue campaign to renovate aging facilities. Over the course of eight months, I spoke with hundreds of diverse community and parent groups about the benefits of this project. We successfully passed this bond initiative with a 70% positive vote.

However, I am most proud of the fact that during my tenure, overall student achievement has risen by over 25 percentage points, with the achievement gaps for children of poverty decreasing. We accomplished this by focusing on alignment of our standards, curriculum, assessments, and professional development program. Good teaching matters, and we provided teachers the support and tools necessary to reach toward professional excellence.

As Deputy, I served on the superintendent's executive leadership team, responsible for overall district management. I was delegated the responsibility for leading the annual budget development process for the district, which has a $75 million annual budget. This included presenting the budget to the Board of Education. I also established our district's accountability plan, which has become a model in our state and is being used by other districts. This was accomplished not by imposing an accountability model on district staff, but by working with them to arrive at a system that would provide meaningful direction and feedback.

I look forward to talking with you about how I could work with Middle City in ensuring that its schools continue to be a positive asset to the entire region in the years ahead. Thank you for giving serious consideration to my application. Please contact me at my home telephone and email address if you have any questions or need further information. Also, please talk with me before contacting any of my references in my current district.

Sincerely,

XXX

Jane Q. Candidate, Ph.D.

Address

City, State Zip

Personal Email Address

Home Phone

Cell Phone

SUMMARY

Experienced educational leader with strong experience in increasing achievement at the secondary level. Member of executive leadership team in a 30,000 student district, with direct responsibility for 5 schools with 6,500 students. Outstanding skills in:

- Increasing rigor and high expectations
- Using data to drive instruction and school improvement
- Community engagement

- Increasing student achievement and closing achievement gaps
- Expanding opportunities for minority students
- Staff development to improve instruction

EDUCATION

Ph.D., Educational Administration, University of the North, College Town, VT, 2005

Masters of Science, Educational Administration, University of the North, 1995

Bachelor of Arts, Vermont State University, Upper Village, VT, 1989
Major: History

Certification
Vermont: *History, Administrator, Superintendent*

PROFESSIONAL EXPERIENCE

Area Superintendent   2007 – Present
Middle City Public Schools, Middle City, VT

Provide leadership to 5 schools serving 6,500 students of this 30,000-student district. (Area supervised includes 1 high school, 1 middle school, 3 elementary schools.) Area has 63% students of poverty, 30% English language learners; 35% of students African American, 30% Hispanic, 5% Asian, and 30% Caucasian.

- Serve on superintendent's executive leadership team, providing input into system strategic goals, budget, and continuous improvement
- Increased reading proficiency in elementary schools by 25 percentage points by implementing standardized reading program
- Implemented retention programs that reduced high school dropout rate from 35% to 10%
- Developed capacities of principals to utilize data and drive achievement in their schools

Principal   2002 – 2007
Stone Henge High School
Stone City Public Schools, Stone City, NH

Provided leadership to a high school serving 2,300 students; 25% economically disadvantaged, 50% African American, 35% Caucasian, 15% Hispanic

- Worked with staff and school community on utilizing data-driven decisions for instructional improvement, resulting in a 25% increase in SAT scores over a five-year period
- 35% increase in number of students graduating having taken at least one AP course; minority student AP participation increased from 10% to 45%
- Served on district-wide strategic planning task force
- Co-chaired bond campaign for construction of new high school

Assistant Principal   1994 – 2002
Washington High School
New Town Public Schools, New Town, MD

Developed and implemented master schedule. Observed and evaluated certificated and support staff. Supervised School Improvement Teams and commencement activities.

Social Studies Teacher   1989 – 1994
Washington High School
New Town Public Schools, New Town, MD

OTHER PROFESSIONAL EXPERIENCE

Adjunct Professor   2006 – 2008
Walden Pond College, Walden, NH

Taught classes in Educational Administration and Instructional Supervision.

AWARDS AND RECOGNITION

- *New Hampshire Principal of the Year*, NHASSP, 2007
- *Buck Stone County Principal of the Year,* Buck Stone County Association for Student Councils, 2005

PROFESSIONAL AND COMMUNITY ACTIVITIES

- Co-Chair, National Association of Secondary School Principals Task Force on the Principal, 2005 – 2006
- Leadership Committee Chairperson, Buck Stone Aspiring Leadership Committee, 2005 – 2007
- United Way Education Committee Chair, Buck Stone Area, 2006

SAMPLE SUPERINTENDENT INTERVIEW QUESTIONS

OPENING QUESTIONS

While we have had the opportunity to review your resume, our audience has not. Would you briefly review your background and employment history?

Could you tell us why you are interested in this position at this point in your career?

What specific capabilities and qualities would you bring to this position that would set you apart from others?

COMMUNITY AND PARENT RELATIONS

What are some examples of community activities in which you have provided leadership, and in what ways did that benefit your district?

Describe an experience in which you faced controversy and community opposition in achieving your goals. How was the situation resolved, and what did you learn from that experience?

Parents are a child's first teachers. Unfortunately, many children today do not have parents who are involved and supportive of their child's education. What specific strategies would you recommend for a school district to take that would remedy that situation?

What examples can you provide where you have personally developed and promoted school partnerships with outside organizations?

What should each parent expect from their child's school?

POLITICAL AWARENESS

What is your opinion of merit pay for teachers?

One of the challenges we face is the possibility of closing some schools. How would you handle that decision-making process? What would be your criteria for closing schools?

What is your view on school choice and charter schools in our district?

What do you believe is the greatest challenge facing urban school districts today, and what do you believe should be done to address that challenge?

There are many constituencies with potentially competing interests in the district—the teachers' union, the board, the business community, parents, and others. As superintendent, how would you go about balancing and addressing these varying interests?

LEADERSHIP ATTRIBUTES

If we asked the board, administrators and staff in your current position about your leadership style and effectiveness, what would they say?

What is the most important responsibility of the superintendent?

Describe a district planning process you believe would be a model to follow.

Talk to us about how you would approach your first 90 days on the job.

Tell us how you define and measure success in your current position and how that might apply to our district.

Describe a situation where you decided to implement a significant change, but it was not supported by one or more staff groups. How did you proceed and what was the outcome?

What are the core values or principles that drive you and your work? Have you ever had a situation in which these values were at risk of being compromised? Please describe what you did and the outcomes.

BOARD/SUPERINTENDENT RELATIONSHIPS

Have you worked with a board, and how did you establish and maintain a good working relationship with the board?

What do you think is the role of the board versus the role of the superintendent? How would you establish and maintain that understanding in working with this board?

If you were hired, what would you expect from the board?

If the board did not approve one of your recommendations, how would you handle that?

How do you envision the board holding you accountable? On what should you be evaluated?

Do you believe it would be better for our district if the mayor rather than the board were the governing authority, and the superintendent reported to the mayor instead?

TEACHING AND LEARNING

How would you go about ensuring that the curriculum in our district was appropriate and aligned with meaningful standards?

What experience and success have you had with coordination of instruction and curriculum that serves the abilities and talents of all children?

What is your experience in improving student achievement as measured by standardized tests? How would you plan to bridge the gap between high and low achieving students?

How is teaching effectiveness best measured?

How is student achievement best measured?

What is the biggest risk you have taken to do what's right for children?

What do you believe are the main challenges and opportunities with special education programs in our district?

What is your philosophy on best serving English Language Learners? What have you found to be effective?

What do you believe is the best and most appropriate role of technology in the education of children?

What would be your strategy for making our high schools more effective in preparing all high school students for success in college and career?

Please tell us what you have done in the area of middle school reform. What has been the result?

FINANCES AND OPERATIONS

Describe your experience with budget development and financial management.

How do you prioritize and budget for art, music, gifted and talented, and athletic programs when budgets are tight?

What needs to be done to ensure that district finances are controlled properly and reported clearly and completely?

What is your experience with cutting budgets while still improving organizational performance? Can it be done?

What has been your experience and track record in procuring district funding beyond state and federal aid and tax levies?

Tell us about your experience with managing capital projects.

To what extent should budget authority be decentralized to the school level?

What has been your experience with management of facilities and other operational areas such as transportation, food service, and other supporting services?

How would you go about holding the various operational areas of the district accountable for high performance?

STAFF AND UNION RELATIONS

How do you delegate responsibility yet hold central office staff and school sites accountable for results?

What strategies would you suggest for providing appropriate professional development for teachers in times of tight budgets?

What would be your approach to developing and assessing the performance of school principals?

What positions would be critical on your executive staff team? What kinds of people would you want on your team?

Please describe your most successful experience in building a high performing work team.

Describe your experience in working with labor unions.

How would you describe your working relationship with your teachers' union president?

Tell us about the last time you fired someone.

What do you believe we should be doing to recruit and retain a more diverse teaching force?

In your current position, how much time do you spend in the schools and in the classrooms? Describe a typical visit.

FINAL BOARD QUESTIONS

What challenges do you foresee in transitioning into this position and into our district?

Why do you believe you will be successful here?

Looking back over your career, what are the two or three accomplishments you are most proud of? In what ways might your performance be criticized?

CANDIDATE QUESTIONS FOR BOARD

What questions do you have for the board?

CLOSING

Do you have a closing statement or is there anything you would like to add?

Part of your entry plan is to meet one-on-one with individual board members. (It is also suggested that superintendents conduct one-on-one interviews with board members annually—if not semi-annually, and always with new members of the board. The format and questions can be adapted for the respective setting.)

Format

These meetings should be scheduled during the first week on the job, if not before your formal start date. If the level of trust in the system is relatively high, it would be good to include a trusted staff person for the sole purpose of taking notes so that you can be fully engaged in the discussion. If trust is low, the interview should be one-on-one, and you should allow time in-between interviews to make your notes and summarize.

The interviews should be scheduled for 90 minutes, which should provide ample time for each board member to feel that they have been heard and understand how you will proceed over your first 90 days. If at all possible, go to the board member at a time and place of their convenience and where they are comfortable.

Introductory Comments

- Thank them for taking the time to share their thoughts, ideas and wisdom with you. Let them know how important you consider their input to be.
- Explain why you're doing this, that this is part of your listening and learning plan.
- Explain the ground rules—that you will not quote them on anything sensitive they might say without requesting their permission to do so.
- Remind them your purpose is to learn as much about the system as you can and to better understand their perspectives regarding the same. State that you will be comparing their thoughts and perspectives with other board members as you attempt to identify themes that will guide you in the coming months.

- Start by sharing appropriate additional information about yourself and your leadership story that you may want them to be aware of—no more than five minutes.
- Share any initial observations you have of the system and the community that might serve as an appropriate backdrop to the interview. Remember to be positive and be constructive.

Questions

- I'd like to begin by asking you to tell me a little about yourself. Go back as far as you'd like and tell me about the key events that led to you having a position on the board.
- How would you describe your board experience to date? Please elaborate on the highlights and challenges.
- When we think about the board and superintendent, I use the term "governance team." Can you tell me how effective the governance team has functioned in the past? What has been part of that past that you'd like to see us continue in the future? As we look to the future, how can we improve upon that past performance?
- From your perspective, when you think about the overall performance of the school system, what is working well and whom do you credit for this success?
- From your perspective, thinking about the overall performance of the system, what is not working well, and to what or to whom do you attribute these shortcomings?
- When you think about the broader community that this system serves, what are the greatest challenges and opportunities that we face?
- In pursuing these opportunities, who are the people either within the system or in the broader community that we will need as allies?
- Identify three people in the community for whom you have the greatest respect and tell me why.
- Who are the community leaders I should be spending time with on a one-on-one basis as I enter this position?
- When you think about the people who comprise the leadership team of the district, (those people on staff who report directly to me,) how would you rate the team's performance overall—A,B,C or F?

- Who are the strongest performers on the team and why? If there are any weak links on the team, who are they and why do you think so?
- If I'm to be successful as your new superintendent, what suggestions or advice can you give me in support of that end?
- Is there anything else that you want me to know?
- Of all the things that you've shared with me today, are there specific items you can think of that you would not want to be quoted on without further discussion with you?
- We have our first governance team retreat scheduled within the next few weeks. What items do you believe we need to talk about as a team to help make sure that this partnership gets off on the right foot?

Closing

If you have any other thoughts following our conversation today that you believe are pertinent, please don't hesitate to contact me.

Make sure that each board member has your private email address and phone number for your private line, if that's a protocol you would like to have.

Plan of Entry
Format for Initial Interviews with Leadership Team Members

Part of your entry plan is to meet one on one with individual members of your leadership team and all direct reports.

Format

These meetings should be scheduled for your first week on the job (if not before your formal start date) but definitely before your first leadership team retreat. The interviews should be conducted in a neutral site if possible, away from interruptions. The interviews should be scheduled for 90 minutes, which will provide ample time for each staff member to feel they have been heard, get a feeling for your expectations, and better understand how you'll proceed in your first 90 days on the job.

These meetings should be preceded by the submission—at your request—of an updated resume so that you can understand the individual within the context of their entire career, and a 3-5 page briefing report on their area of responsibility which highlights:
  a) significant accomplishments during their tenure,
  b) particular challenges of their role,
  c) issues on the horizon which have the potential to create special challenges for the system, and
  d) their aspirations and interests.

Introductory Comments

- Thank them for taking the time to update their resume, create their briefing report, and meet with you.
- Explain that you're conducting interviews with each member of the leadership team as part of your listening and learning plan. Your objective is to get to know them better, to better understand their accomplishments and aspirations, and understand any special challenges where you may be of support.
- Explain the ground rules—that you will not quote anything they say without their permission to do so.
- Let them know you'll be comparing their thoughts and perspectives with others with whom you'll be meeting, including other members of the leadership team, in an attempt to identify themes that will guide you in the coming months.

- Start by sharing any appropriate additional information about yourself you want them to be aware of—no more than five minutes.
- Share any initial observations you have of the community and the system that might serve as an appropriate backdrop to the interview.
- Remember, be positive and be constructive.

Questions

- I've had the opportunity to review your resume, but I would like to hear you tell me more about yourself in your own words. Go back as far as you'd like in your life and tell me about the key events that led you to your current role in the system.
- How would you describe your experience here to date?
- Tell me about the accomplishments you are most proud of since you've been here.
- When you think about districts our size around the state that are generally considered to be "the best," how would you compare your area of responsibility with your peers' in those districts?
- Talk to me about the challenges in your particular area of responsibility.
- As you've attempted to make improvements, have there been any barriers placed in your path by my office, the board, the community, or any constituent groups?
- Tell me what your relationship, if any, has been with the board up to this point.
- If you were starting as the superintendent, what would be high on your list of things that need to be fixed quickly?
- What kinds of special challenges do you see in the weeks, months, or year ahead in your area of responsibility? How can I be of help to you?
- Talk to me about your career plans. Where would you like to be in five years?
- How many years do you have in the state retirement system?
- Are there any family issues that have implications for your work in this district, either short or long term—i.e. retirement or job transfer of spouse, etc.?
- Is there anything else you want me to be aware of as we move forward in our relationship?

Plan of Entry
Format for Initial Interviews with Community Leaders

Part of your entry plan is to meet one-on-one with key individuals in the community who are instrumental to the system's success. These are the opinion leaders and people who can either kill or advance your agenda within their constituent groups—and perhaps with your board. Names of people to interview will arise during your interviews with board members. As you conduct these meetings, be looking for members of your "kitchen cabinet."

Format

These meetings should be scheduled beginning with your appointment and throughout your first 60 days on the job. You may choose to include a trusted staff person in the meetings for the sole purpose of taking notes so that you can be fully engaged in the discussion.

The interviews should be scheduled for one hour, which should provide ample time for each person to get to know you, to feel that they have been heard and to better understand what they can expect from you as their new superintendent. If at all possible, appointments should be scheduled at their office or other place of convenience to them.

Introductory Comments

- Thank them for taking the time to share their thoughts, ideas and wisdom with you. Let them know how important you consider their input to be.
- Explain why you're doing this, that this is part of your listening and learning plan.
- Explain the ground rules—that you will not quote them on anything sensitive they might say without requesting their permission to do so.
- Remind them your purpose is to learn as much about the system and community as you can and to better understand their perspectives regarding the same. State that you will be comparing their thoughts and perspectives with other key community leaders as you attempt to identify themes that will guide you in the coming months.

- Start by sharing an appropriate amount of information about yourself, and what led you to pursuit and acceptance of this position—no more than five minutes.
- Share any initial observations you have of the system and the community that might serve as an appropriate backdrop to the interview. Remember to be positive and be constructive.

Questions

- Could you talk a little bit about how long you've been in the community, and how you have been engaged with the schools?
- When you think about the overall school system and its performance, how would you rate the system—A, B, C or F? Can you talk about why you gave the system the rating that you did?
- When you think about the history of this system, could you talk to me about key events you recall that have been significant in bringing the system to the point where it is today?
- When you think about governance of this system, could you share your perceptions of our board of education and how effectively they work together to advance the agenda for our children?
- When you think about our governance team, are there individuals who stand out in your mind? Who are they, and why?
- When we think about policy makers including governmental officials and legislators, who among them are most influential and most important for the system to have as allies as we proceed?
- Have you had the opportunity to spend any time with the individuals who are direct reports to the superintendent? Are there any impressions that you'd like to share that may be of value to me as I enter this role?
- When you think about the broader community, who are the individuals with whom I should spend some time with, besides yourself, to solicit their thinking on the district's future?
- As you think about the future of the system, and the community working together, what are the primary objectives that we should be pursuing?
- (If the interviewee is a representative of the private sector) How good of a job has the system done in preparing graduates to serve the needs of your business? Provide examples if possible.
- As I begin my position as superintendent of schools, what general advice would you offer to me?

- May I call upon you for additional thoughts and advice as I proceed in the superintendency?

Closing

Should you have any thoughts regarding the school system that you think might be helpful to me as I begin this role, please don't hesitate to contact me. I want to thank you for your time, guidance, and wisdom, and for all that you've done for the system to this point, and for your continued support.

ABOUT THE AUTHORS

Timothy Quinn

Dr. Timothy G. Quinn's career spans teaching and leadership at all levels of public education from K-12 through community college and university. He served as an English teacher, assistant principal, and principal in Michigan, prior to becoming superintendent of the Green Bay Public Schools and serving a term as Wisconsin's Deputy State Superintendent of Instruction. He also served as president of Northwestern Michigan College in Traverse City, Michigan, and was designated President Emeritus upon his departure—only the second president in the college's history to be granted that status. Dr. Quinn was then appointed by The University of Michigan as chief executive officer of Michigan's first virtual college.

Tim was the founder and is president emeritus of the highly successful Michigan Leadership Institute, which is dedicated to leadership development, placement of outstanding leaders, and continuous research on the topic of leadership. As a result of the Institute's work, Tim was engaged by The Eli and Edythe Broad Foundation to partner on the creation of The Broad Center for the Management of School Systems and the Broad Superintendents Academy.

Having been raised on a hog farm in an Irish family with 10 kids, Tim's first leadership position came at the age of seven—when his father appointed him Director of Manure Management. He is now a farmer once again, in northern Michigan, and is the proud father of two educators, with five grandchildren.

Tim earned a Ph.D. in educational leadership from The University of Michigan, and received honorary doctoral degrees for his statewide leadership from Eastern Michigan, Central Michigan and Grand Valley State Universities.

Michelle (Shelley) Keith

Michelle E. Keith's career includes twenty years of higher education experience in the areas of human resources, planning and governance. As a human resources administrator at Iowa State University and as the Director of Human Resources at Northwestern Michigan College, she has had extensive experience in recruitment, employment, and professional development.

Shelley was the co-founder and former vice president of the Michigan Leadership Institute, and was engaged by The Eli and Edythe Broad Foundation to partner on the creation and management of the Broad Superintendents Academy.

She has a bachelor's degree and master's degree from Iowa State University.

Made in the USA
Columbia, SC
08 September 2017